Beanie Baby® Stories

**BEANIE BABY® STORIES**
IS NOT CONNECTED WITH TY, Inc.

*Beanie Baby® Stories* is not authorized
or licensed by TY, Inc.

# Beanie Baby® ❤❤❤❤❤ Stories

COMPILED BY

## Susan Titus Osborn & Sandra Jensen

STARBURST PUBLISHERS®
*Lancaster, Pennsylvania*

To schedule author appearances, write: Author Appearances, Starburst Promotions, P.O. Box 4123, Lancaster, Pennsylvania 17604 or call (717) 293-0939. Website: www.starburstpublishers.com.

CREDITS:
Cover design by David Marty Design
Text design and composition by John Reinhardt Book Design

To the best of its ability, Starburst Publishers has strived to find the source of all material. If there has been an oversight, please contact us and we will make any correction deemed necessary in future printings. We also declare that to the best of our knowledge all material (quoted or not) contained herein is accurate, and we shall not be held liable for the same.

First Printing, April, 1999
ISBN: 1-892016-04-4
Library of Congress Catalog Number: 98-83166
Printed in the United States of America

Ty, Beanie Babies®, and all Beanie Baby® names are registered trademarks of Ty, Inc. Teenie Beanies® is a registered trademark of Ty, Inc. and the McDonald's Corporation. Beanie Baby® Stories is not in any way associated or endorsed by Ty, Inc.

# Contents

❤ ❤ ❤

❤ v ❤

## Contents

## Contents

# ❤ Contents ❤

# Introduction

♥ ♥ ♥

**S**ome people pick on Beanie Babies; they say a Beanie Baby is just a bunch of plastic pellets bagged up and covered with a bit of fabric. But the people who say so have forgotten the great importance of being a kid, of playing, of having the courage to find magic in something that others overlook.

Then there are those who know better—those who have held a Beanie Baby in wide-eyed wonder, who have made friends with Beanie Babies, those who have started families of Beanie Babies.

More and more people can't seem to get enough of these loveable, little animals. Beanie Babies are everywhere—perching on computers, peeking from backpacks, and lounging on dashboards.

This book is full of stories about how Beanie Babies have truly made a difference in the lives of both the young *and* the young at heart. You'll read, for example, how Valentino the bear taught a brother and sister the importance of giving. You'll discover how a girl and her Beanie Babies raised over a thousand dollars for Red Cross. You'll find out how Freckles the baby leopard turned prejudice into acceptance. Beanie Babies are making the world a better place!

In addition to the stories, children's drawings add a special, playful look, and surprising trivia will make you sit back and think. There's something for everybody here!

We found ourselves laughing, crying, and pondering as we gathered together these heartwarming stories. We know you'll enjoy reading them as much as we did, but here's a word to the wise . . . read with a child's heart.

SUSAN TITUS OSBORN AND SANDRA JENSEN
*Editors*

# The Perfect Pets

BY KAREN O'CONNOR

❤ ❤ ❤

"I want a dog," I told my husband Charles last November. "Really?" he asked, raising his eyebrows. "I'm surprised. I thought we agreed a dog wouldn't work in our condo."

"True," I said, remembering the reasons we had listed. No yard. Carpeted floors. We both work. Vet bills. Food. Shots. Housebreaking. The list went on.

"I guess I'm feeling sentimental," I said. "I want something cute and cuddly to curl up with on the sofa."

My husband looked hurt. "You've told me I'm cute," he said, "and I love to cuddle."

We laughed, hugged, and scrapped the dog idea once again.

Six weeks later on Christmas Eve, Charles presented me with a huge box from Nordstrom where he works.

I tore into the wrappings like an excited child. Beneath layers of snow-white tissue were two of the cutest and cuddliest stuffed dogs I had ever seen! I burst out crying on the spot. "Oh Charles, they're wonderful," I said, leaping into his lap and covering his face with kisses.

"Down girl," he joked. "You said you wanted a dog,

didn't you? Well, they're small, neat, and very obedient so I got two—one for you and one for me. And they're, well, cute and cuddly, too. Pet them."

I pulled them close and nuzzled my face into their soft fur.

I plopped Dotty on my lap, and Charles grabbed Bruno. We relaxed on our favorite sofa with our two new dogs resting comfortably on our chests.

That night I put our perfect pets in a little breadbasket, nestled on a soft towel, at the foot of our bed. They remained there without a whimper—until we took them out.

Two months later upon returning from a business trip, I ran into our bedroom to greet the dogs. Something was different. I saw two tiny heads poking over the rim of the basket. "What's this?" I asked.

"Take a look," said Charles with a mischievous grin. I lifted up the big dogs and underneath were two adorable puppies, Doby who was dark like Bruno, and Bones who resembled Dotty with his sad eyes and droopy ears.

"Beanie Baby® puppies," I yelled. "How did they get here?"

"It just happened," said my husband with a twinkle in his eye. "I guess Dotty and Bruno were together in that basket a little too long!"

# The Gift of Giving

## BY DENISE MITCHELL

❤ ❤ ❤

Six months ago we took our four children on a trip to Ventura, California, where we attended a Beanie Baby show. Afterwards we spent the night at a beachfront hotel with a wonderful view of the Pacific Ocean.

The following day we rented a bicycle cart that allowed our entire family to ride together. We pedaled down the bike path along the beach. When we stopped to rest, we saw a man and a woman pushing a boy, probably in his late teens, in a bed-type wheelchair. He appeared to be a paraplegic.

My kids waved as we went by. Then my son Kevin suggested, "Let's go to the van and get a Beanie Baby for the boy. I bet he'd enjoy that."

"That's a great idea," I agreed, appreciating how thoughtful my children were.

My daughter Stacy said, "Let's give him Princess."

Kevin and I looked at each other with a questioning look. I said, "Let's be sure to give him a Beanie that he will really like. We like Princess, but what would he like?

When we got to the van the kids rummaged through the

*Catrina Kingsbury*

many boxes and finally found Valentino. Stacy read the poem on the hangtag.

It says that Valentine's heart is bursting with love and keep him close if you're sad because he has much love to give.

After she finished, Stacy got tears in her eyes.

I put my arm around her and asked, "What's wrong, honey?"

She said, "I never knew how much that bear or that poem meant until I thought about giving Valentino to the boy on the beach."

Seeing my daughter's compassion brought tears to my eyes.

We locked the van and peddled back to the beach where the boy and his parents had been, but they were gone.

Kevin said, "Let's peddle fast and try to find him."

Before long we found them farther down the beach on the bike path. The kids ran up to the boy. Stacy handed him Valentino and said, "This is a special bear just for you. Please read the poem on his hangtag."

The parents thanked all of us, appreciation reflecting in their eyes.

We all climbed back on the bicycle cart and peddled away. I had tears in my eyes, and my kids had big smiles on their faces!

Being avid collectors, we always thought Beanies were so important to own. But that day on the beach we discovered they are even better to give away!

# The Beanie Legacy

## BY SALLY JADLOW

❤ ❤ ❤

"Inoperable." The word hung in the air like a death sentence. My adult daughter, Jennifer, had just been diagnosed with a tumor inside her spinal column. Cancer or not, it had to come out, but we were unable to find a local doctor to operate.

In time we learned of a doctor in New York City who would attempt to remove the tumor. The week before Jennifer left for New York, she went shopping for presents for her three children. She decided upon Beanie Babies as the perfect gifts.

When I arrived at Jennifer's house to take care of the children while she was gone, she said, "Mom, I want you to come upstairs. I have something to show you." She opened her dresser drawer and carefully pulled out fifteen Beanie Babies. "I want you to give Jordan the following Beanies: Weenie, Grunt, Congo, Bongo, and Spike. Give Brooke Ringo, Bernie, Lucky, Fleece, and Zip. Also give little Gunnar Spot, Blackie, Floppity, Wrinkles and Twigs."

"When am I supposed to give these animals to the kids?" I asked.

"Give them each one tomorrow after I leave for New York. Give them the second one after you hear I'm out of surgery. As the days wear on and you can tell they're missing me, give them more."

There was a long pause before she spoke again. "Save one Beanie Baby for each of them until the day I come home or . . ."

I looked at my daughter and suddenly realized we might be talking face-to-face for the last time here on earth. I could tell she sensed the same thing.

It was a month to the day that my dear Jennifer returned home to her family. After a tearful reunion she directed me to retrieve the three remaining Beanies from her drawer. She handed Congo to Jordan and Fleece to Brooke, and gave Blackie to Gunnar. The kids threw their arms around their mom, while holding tightly to their new Beanies.

I looked at my daughter, realizing the miracle that had taken place and said a silent prayer. *Thank You, God, for this gift. I have my daughter home again.*

> My favorite Beanie is Pugsly. I love Pugsly because I own a pug dog, and her name is Phoebe. I love her curly tail.
>
> Submitted by Blake Leonhardt (age 9)

# I Need Peace!

BY DELL SMITH KLEIN

💜 💜 💜

During the night, it rained. From my bedroom window, I could see that I had left the car windows open. The upholstery probably was ruined. Before breakfast, my daughter called to say she had dropped out of college to join a singing group. An hour later, my husband called to tell me he had invited one of his customers over for dinner.

The whole morning, as I dusted and readied the house for company, all I could think of was soggy car seats and a girl giving up her future for a song.

That afternoon my daughter-in-law came by to drop off grandchildren without calling first. She said that she knew I'd be thrilled to have them for a little while.

But baby Bethany was cranky and, because of the rain, four-year-old Brittany couldn't play outside. The day's events kept playing in my head. Even a dinner menu eluded me. I felt like any moment I might shatter into a million pieces.

"God," I prayed, "what I really need is a little peace!"

"Grandma, can we play with your Beanie Babies?" Brittany asked.

"Sure." The children loved my small collection. It might keep them busy for a while and allow me to gather my thoughts. I pulled down my box and dumped the contents on the couch. Even the baby smiled as she crawled toward the colorful critters. While they played, I poured myself a cup of tea and sat in the rocking chair, next to a window that looked out at the cloud-shrouded mountains.

"Here Grandma. Here's one for you." Brittany handed me a funny little tie-dyed bear.

Curious, I looked at the name on its tag. Peace, I read. Peace. Exactly what I needed on a day like this.

---

More Mistakes: On the Internet Jeannine Twardus reported a misspelled word in the poem of Chops the Lamb—"surly" appeared instead of "curly." A similar mistake occurred with Hoot the Owl—"quite" was spelled as "qutie." Ms. Twardus quipped, "I hope Chops is surely not a 'surly' lamb! And Hoot, although he's a cutie 'qutie,' I like to think of him as 'quite' wise!"

# The Beanie Push

## BY GERRI BROWN

❤ ❤ ❤

As principal of an elementary school in Vacaville, California, I work with many students who are struggling in school. Teachers send students to me when they complete their work, or do a great job on an assignment. This gives them the opportunity to view the principal's office as a positive place to visit.

About four weeks ago one of my second grade teachers talked to me about a boy in her class. I'll call him "Jason."

"Jason spends most of his day with his head on the desk crying or sleeping. I'm tremendously worried about him," she said.

I felt concerned, too. I suggested that she send him to see me with *any* work he completed so that I could make a fuss over him and let him know how proud I was of him. She did, and after looking over his papers, he and I even shared his work with the assistant principal and the secretaries.

He seemed to like that, and a couple of days later he came back to see me again. This time I let him pick a prize out of my treasure box. He really liked that idea, too.

His teacher told me that the tears were less frequent, and he was trying much harder.

The second week I happened to have my new Beanie Baby, Peace, sitting on a shelf in my office when Jason came to visit me. He saw the bear and asked, "Can I have it?"

"I'm sorry, Jason," I replied. "It's my special bear, so I can't give it to you."

Jason thought for a moment and then asked, "Can I earn a Beanie Baby of my own."

I studied the young student for a moment. "You'll have to show me a lot more papers that you've completed in class before I will buy you a Beanie of your own."

Being a smart little guy he asked, "How long do I have to bring you good papers in order to get my Beanie?"

I replied, "Two weeks, and I need to see work every day, Jason."

Wow! Did he accept the challenge. Every day for two weeks he was in my office to show me his reading or math, sometimes both! How proud he was of himself, and how proud his teacher and I were of him.

On Monday he came in with a smile and another math paper. That smile grew even bigger when I told him, "Look on the shelf, Jason, and pick the Beanie Baby you want."

He picked Doby. What a big hug he gave his new friend!

Jason hasn't missed a day this week bringing in his schoolwork. He is now negotiating for his next prize.

I figure if a Beanie Baby will help motivate a student to try rather than give up it is well worth the money. And it proves that children can learn—some may just need a little Beanie push!

# Glory's Gift

## BY BECKY DILLON

♥ ♥ ♥

**E**leven-year-old Cody Davis knows moms are more important than Beanie Babies. Cody, who lives in Montrose, Colorado, keeps most of his collection of Beanie Babies in plastic bags, hoping to cash them in for college money. His prize Beanie Baby was a special edition bear named Glory that his grandparents brought back from the all-star game in Denver this year.

When Cody's mom, Nancy, was diagnosed with breast cancer, he didn't hesitate to help out however he could. His grandma's idea to auction off one of his Beanie Babies seemed fine to him. He wrote letters to the editors of several Colorado newspapers to let people know about his auction.

The response was overwhelming! Thousands of dollars of donations, as well as bids and offers for donations of more Glory bears, came in from all across the United States.

Cody was even asked to appear on *The Rosie O'Donnell Show* and *The Montel Williams Show*. Although those invitations didn't pan out, the auction raised about $10,000 toward his mom's stem-cell treatment. Cody eventually sent

*Stephanie Kodosky*

the bear to a cancer survivor in Nebraska who placed the highest bid of $2,000. The Davis family plans to use the additional donated bears at auctions to raise money for local cancer groups.

It's been a big year for Cody, who just re-entered public school in September after being homeschooled for the past few years. In a way, the attention from the auction has been a welcome distraction. Yet, the family is also trying to keep things as normal as possible while Nancy goes through chemotherapy and other medical treatments.

"Cody is 'tickled' with the funds that are still streaming in," Nancy said. "He nearly fainted when he opened an envelope with a $1,000 donation check from a man in Texas."

Throughout the fundraising efforts, the whole family has been astonished by the generosity of individuals around the country.

"It's made a lasting impression on Cody. This experience has made him aware that there are lots of good folks in the world who are willing to help others in need," Nancy said, beaming.

A complete set of twelve Teenie Beanie Babies recently went for as much as $200. These miniature replicas of the original bean-bag animals created by H. Ty Warner brought mob-like crowds to McDonald's restaurants nationwide in 1997; the toys sold out three weeks before the promotion was over.

# Lessons from a Baby

## BY SARAH GROUX (AGE 15)

❤ ❤ ❤

I was at my aunt's house one day when I noticed my eighteen-month-old cousin playing with something furry. I looked over and saw that the baby was holding Nuts the squirrel. And the swing tag was in her mouth! I panicked.

Everyone who knows Beanie Babies knows that they lose their value if the tags are removed. I ran over and took the tag out of her mouth (I didn't want her to choke), and then I picked up the Beanie Baby and examined it. It was a mess—no swing tag, grimy and dirty, slobbery from the baby chewing on it. Worst of all, there was a hole in its tail. I cringed, having never seen a Beanie look so bad. I took it over to the sink and started wiping off the stains.

Suddenly, I felt a tug on my shorts. I looked down and saw my adorable baby cousin reaching for her Beanie Baby. In that moment it dawned on me that I was acting rather "hyper" about this child's toy. Without a second thought, I handed her the little stuffed squirrel. She took it back gleefully.

After that experience, I decided that I am free to collect and treasure my Beanie Babies®, but I should not "freak out" when I see a little one loving her cuddly critter any way she pleases.

*Michael Evans, age 10*

# Higgins Approves

BY DIANE NEAL

❤ ❤ ❤

**H**iggins is a very particular cat. He is a sable Burmese and the runt of his litter. He is both clawless and clueless as far as street smarts go. He sees himself as a friendly panther who has consented to live with my husband and me. According to Higgins, he owns everything in his domain and must approve each object that is brought into the house.

"He keeps a tight inventory," my son Jarod said as Higgins leaped up on the dining room table to examine a painting that previously had been stored in the garage.

One day I brought a small, white sack into the house and put it on the table. Higgins quickly appeared out of thin air as he often does when new objects invade his territory. A smooth leap brought him within stalking distance, and he crouched, making his way carefully along the crocheted tablecloth. Suddenly he pounced on the offending sack and caught it unaware.

A few swipes of his paw, and out came a soft, round object. He shoved his way into the sack. Out came another fluffy object! Higgins had found the beautiful, red ladybug Beanie Baby I had bought for my granddaughters, Nicole and Haley.

The sniff test came first. He carefully smelled at each Lucky as he gingerly turned the ladybugs around with his foot. Being color blind, he could not appreciate their deep, red color, but he could see their black spots. They seemed harmless enough at first sight, but he was taking no chances. They bore no resemblance to cats, which would have required much greater scrutiny. He pressed Lucky's red back to see if there was a reaction. No, nothing there. He batted it with his paw. Again, no reaction. At last, he decided the Beanie Babies posed no threat. He grudgingly rubbed each with his cheek, marking them with his approval.

We breathed a sigh of relief. They were accepted. We could keep them.

*Aaron Rucker, age 8*

# A Beanie Transition

## BY JERI CHRYSONG

♥ ♥ ♥

**A**s a condolence when my cocker spaniel Dudley died, my friend bought me Spunky the cocker spaniel Beanie Baby. Unexpectedly, this little Beanie's soulful expression comforted me, and I slept with him for many nights. In time, my family's sorrow lessened, and I knew that sooner or later I'd have to find another dog to fill the void created by Dudley's departure.

I studied different breeds, their pluses and minuses, and for various reasons, settled on a Pug—mainly because a Pug is quite different than a cocker spaniel. We even purchased Pugsly the Pug Beanie in anticipation of our live puppy's arrival.

We named our young pug Puddy, a cross between Pug and Buddy. He was so tiny, barely larger than Pugsly! On our outings, children would often say, "Look, Mommy, there's Pugsly!" Even Puddy himself seemed to recognize Pugsly, possibly mistaking him for one of his brothers he'd recently left behind. He always made a dash for Pugsly, over Spunky and the "other dogs," for something to chew on.

Puddy's abbreviated nose took some getting used to as well as his curly tail. His tiny ears reminded me of little pieces of velvet, so different from Dudley's long, silky spaniel ears. But then, I had wanted a dog much different.

Owning two such unusual dogs has made me appreciate God's creativity in assigning such unique characteristics to each breed, and I marvel at how Ty, the creator of the Beanie Babies, has captured those characteristics in each animal. I will always be grateful for how Beanie Baby puppies helped smooth the way for my family as we made the transition from one special pet to the next.

# Moose Encounter

## BY BETTY SHAFFER

❤ ❤ ❤

Looking over a Beanie Baby display one day, a sprawling moose caught my eye. I immediately bought Chocolate for our friend Bill. We had camped with him and his family in the Grand Tetons years ago.

Looking at that little critter triggered some terrific memories! I remembered loading up our gear in the canoe and paddling up String Lake with the rocky bottom shimmering through the clear water. We set up camp in the wilderness site for which we had begged a permit. I could still smell the scent of lodge pine where we set up our green canvas umbrella tent. But the image that remained the clearest in my mind was the view of Mt. Moran reflected in Leigh Lake, its waters so pure we used it for drinking.

Delivering the adorable moose with his yellow antlers to Bill and his wife, we relived our moose adventure. Bill and my husband laughed as they told the story, though it wasn't funny at the time.

We thought back to the evening when the men set off to go fishing. Tramping along an easy trail on the side of the mountain, they were suddenly confronted by a moose. The huge animal spied them about the same time they saw him. He started toward them as they desperately sought a way of escape. But there wasn't a tree in sight! There were only low growing shrubs that the moose had been dining on. He grew bigger with every step toward them. Suddenly he stopped, lowered his head, shook his broad massive antlers, and pawed the ground. Their hearts pounded.

There was nothing to do but retreat. Fearful of rousing the massive animal further, they controlled their urge to run and backed gingerly away, keeping their eyes on him. Placing one foot carefully behind the other, time seemed to stop. What could they do if he decided to attack? Fishing rods make poor weapons.

At last the bull turned his side to them. They held their breath as he lowered his head, exposing the hump on his back, and continued grazing. A thankful pair made it safely back to our flickering campfire. No fish for breakfast, but no one cared!

Chocolate the moose perches on the back of Bill's sofa. He's a welcome reminder of our wilderness experience and a non-threatening figure who requires no retreat.

Ty products include Ty Beanie Babies, Ty Collectibles, Ty Plush Collections, and the new Ty Beanie Buddies.

# The Would-be Easter Bunny

BY RONICA STROMBERG

❤ ❤ ❤

**W**hen my son was two years old, Grandma gave him a Beanie Baby named Floppity. The lavender bunny had long, plush hair, and I thought it would make the perfect prop for an Easter photo.

Wanting to keep Floppity in good shape until I could have it photographed with my son, I tucked it out of sight amongst the twenty-or-so other stuffed animals he had collected in his room. I thought he would soon forget about it.

Wrong. Shortly after Grandma left, he began asking for the bunny. I tried pawning off another bunny on him, but he waved it away. It was mere moments until his chubby little fingers uncovered Floppity and latched onto it.

My son and his bunny were basically inseparable from that point on. He named it Carrots, not caring what the red tag said since he was too young to read anyway. He carried it wherever he went, took it to bed at night, and even burped it and cradled it like a baby!

I felt dismayed seeing Floppity grow less and less photogenic —its ears pressed askew and its fur roughed up and matted. But I also recognized it was serving a purpose far more important than it would have as a photographic prop. My son had bonded with the bunny. He was developing a nurturing ability I had been led to believe little boys didn't have.

Who was it that said little boys are "made of snips and snails and puppy dog tails"?

Obviously, someone whose son never had a Beanie Baby!

# Isaiah's Beanies

### BY DEE HODAPP

In March of 1994 we brought home from the hospital a little two-month-old boy who weighed only four pounds. We planned to adopt Isaiah although he was born two months premature and tested positive for crack/cocaine. Half of his brain had been destroyed by his mother's drug use. His medical problems were a mile long, and the doctors tried to talk us out of adopting him. From the first moment I carried Isaiah in the front door our whole family made sure that life revolved around our new little addition.

My husband Mike sells computer software, so he works at home. Several times a year, though, he attends trade shows. Three months after we brought Isaiah home, we went to a homeschooling convention. I was fortunate to have a sitter for our other children, but we did take Isaiah.

Mike was busy selling his computer software, so I spent time walking around with the baby so he could sleep. Over coffee I met a wonderful lady named Sue, who owns a bookstore in Denver, Colorado. Several times I stopped by her booth, and we talked. On the second day of the convention

*Jessica Freitas, age 7*

she stopped me and said, "Look what I just got into my store. They are so cute." She went on and on and showed me some Beanie Babies.

Not only were they darling, but more importantly, Isaiah was able to hold them. At five months of age Isaiah was unable to do most things a five month old could do. In fact he was having a difficult time doing things a newborn could do. But those Beanies brought a smile to his face that melted our hearts. By the end of the convention I had bought over twenty Beanies. And of course being a good mother I promptly removed all the little heart-shaped tags so that Isaiah would not get hurt. Did I save them? No, they were just toys to us. But over the years Isaiah's collection of Beanie Babies grew and grew.

I kept the Beanies in a big plastic bag. Isaiah would always become so excited when I pulled the bag out. He liked me to pour them over the top of him, and he would lay under all those Beanies and laugh and giggle. Our little five-pound bundle became an avid Beanie collector. For his third birthday he received nothing but Beanies.

We lost Isaiah last year. His little body was just too sick to continue. So now his Beanies are all in a curio, and his brothers and sisters help me keep his collection as current as possible. In fact all I received for my last birthday was Beanies. Who would have guessed that little Isaiah would pick a toy that would become such a collector's item.

I know that if Isaiah was here today, he would still be playing with his Beanie Babies. They are perfect for children to play with and love. When I look at the curio and see all of Isaiah's cuddly Beanies, I remember the beautiful smiles and giggles they brought to our special little son.

# Disguised Mom Nabs Final Teenie Beanie Baby

### BY TRISH HOPPER

**M**y children and I fell in love with Beanie Babies last Christmas and have been collecting them since. They bring us joy, laughs, and adventures. Let me tell you about one of our adventures.

During the Teenie Beanie Baby craze we seriously tried to collect a whole set of the Teenies for each one of us. But we never realized what a tough endeavor that would be. As most Beanie Baby fans know, only McDonald's offers Teenie Beanie Babies, but the fast food restaurants in our area seemed to sell out of the beanbag critters before we could get there. Frustration set in big time.

I decided to gather up the kids and ride over to New York State, which is only minutes from our house, though I was sure I wouldn't find a McDonald's with Teenie Beanies still available. By now, it was several weeks into the promotion.

Up ahead we spotted a tiny McDonald's set off from the road in the first small town we came to. They still had the

Teenie Beanie Baby sign up, and since the kids were actually hungry, we decided to go in and have Happy Meals®.

I was surprised that there weren't more people in line. We were so excited by the time we ordered our food I couldn't think straight.

"Do you still have the last three Teenie Beanies available," I asked the girl behind the counter.

When she said "Yes," I was thrilled! But then I saw the sign behind her. "Only one Teenie Beanie Baby per Happy Meal® per customer each day till gone." I groaned. There were only three of us, and we all needed the last three Teenies. I could clearly see them behind the counter in the few remaining boxes. I felt like they were beckoning me to take them home.

We ate our Happy Meals® in silence. Each of the kids wondered who would be the lucky one to end up with the complete set of Teenies while the others would have to make do with an incomplete set.

That's when the idea hit me. I'd order again, but the next time I'd be in disguise! *Yes*, I thought, *it could work*. All we'd have to do is go home and change our clothes and come back for dinner. I said nothing to the kids, but finished lunch quietly.

Later that day, I asked the kids if they'd like to go back to McDonald's for dinner, and they both agreed it would be cool to eat out twice in one day. They didn't even argue the point of changing their clothes.

Everything was going as planned. I felt like a spy in dis-

Charlie the chunky chicken
By Adam Rucker
11/24/98

*Adam Rucker, age 11*

guise as we made our way back to the same McDonald's just hours later. Grinning like a Cheshire cat and convinced that no one would recognize us, we all trooped in and ordered Happy Meals® again for dinner, and, just as I had planned, we each received one of the last three Teenie Beanie Babies.

*Perfect*, I thought. *No one recognized us.* The truth is, I didn't recognize anyone either. Hmmmm . . . maybe the staff had changed for the night-shift—different workers on a different schedule. This was going even smoother than I'd thought.

Still grinning to myself, we finished our meal and walked into the parking lot. Each of the kids now had the Beanies they needed to complete their sets. But, alas, I was still missing the last Teenie. *Oh well*, I thought. *I'll live without it.*

As I was pulling out of the parking lot the thought occurred to me that I could stop at the take-out window. No doubt, there would be a different worker there, too. I quickly tried to alter my appearance. I took off my glasses and put them on the dash. I pulled my long wavy hair back into a tight bun, yanked the sun visor down, and put my arm up in front of my face so the drive-up clerk couldn't get a good look at me.

By this time my kids were looking at me as if I were a little crazy. They kept whispering, "What're you doing, Mom? Why did you take your glasses off. We're not gonna crash, are we?"

I hissed at them to sit down and explained that I was ordering food for tomorrow's lunch. They quieted down but still continued to look at me as if I were a bit loony.

I barely looked at the woman who took my order, and I waited anxiously for the food. I felt so guilty by now I couldn't even swallow. I silently lectured myself for being so devious and continued to wait barely able to breathe.

My palms became sweaty. *I'm going to get caught*, I kept thinking, *How will I explain this to my children, family, and friends.* A jailbird over Teenie Beanie Babies! How could I do this?

Finally, the clerk returned and handed me the Happy Meals® I had ordered. She smiled broadly and looked at me directly. *Oh no, this is it*, I thought. *She's recognized me*!

I took the bags from her hands. With one foot on the gas pedal I was ready to execute a quick retreat. But before I could escape, she looked me right in the eye and said, "You know, this is the most fun I've had in a long time. You must really want these Teenies, huh?"

Looking up at her as innocently as I could, I replied, "Yes, I'm collecting them for the whole family. We're avid Beanie collectors."

However, I was unprepared for her final comment: "Actually, we all rather enjoyed watching you take off your glasses and pull your hair back so we wouldn't recognize you. We've had quite a few crazy collectors in here, but we think the spy routine is the cutest we've seen. In fact, that's why the manager told me to give you the second set of Teenies. You made our day!"

Then, and only then, did I realize that this McDonald's had a camera aimed at the take-out window. They had watched me as I disguised my appearance and waited anxiously for my order.

Well, I did get my complete set of Teenies, after all. But was my face red for hours afterwards. Even the kids giggled all the way home at "Mommy being caught." I don't know if I'll ever live that one down!

# Night of the Beanies

## BY LILLIAN HIGGS (AGE 9)

❤ ❤ ❤

It was a dark and stormy night. Seriously, it really was a dark and stormy night. I'm Snip, you know, the Beanie Baby. I belong to Lilly.

I was curled up, as usual, with my fellow Beanies. Just as Lilly drifted off to sleep, we woke up.

*Lillian Higgs*

*Lillian Higgs*

All of us cats filed downstairs and went into the kitchen for some grub. Nip and Zip looked for popcorn. Chip was busy making cookies. Flip went right for the cat food.

I joined Pounce and Prance on a quest to eat the leftover chicken. Nip and Zip got their paws on popcorn and popped us a bowl. Then we sat down and watched "The Princess Bride."

Smack in the middle of the movie, we heard footsteps.
"Freeze!" Velvet the panther shouted. "Lilly's coming!"
"I think it's time she found out about us," I said.
Lilly turned the corner into the living room and gasped!
"Want to watch the movie with us?" I asked.
"Sure," she whispered, catching her breath.
By the time the movie was over, all of us were asleep.
Later, when Lilly woke up on the couch, she remembered

*Lillian Higgs*

what had happened. "Was I dreaming or were my Beanies talking to me?" she asked.

We didn't answer, so she took us upstairs and put us to bed. After she went back to sleep, we smiled and winked at each other.

*Lillian Higgs*

# The Magic of Mystic

## BY SHARA DARKE

❤ ❤ ❤

I was at a Hallmark store with my six-month-old daughter one day, immensely enjoying the adorable stage where babies talk to everything they see—human or inanimate, living animal or stuffed—it didn't matter to her. As we walked by a shelf with Beanie Babies she reached out in delight.

She immediately chose her favorite Beanie and struck up a conversation with it. Mystic, the unicorn, was the lucky choice. Perhaps she chose him because of his shiny horn! It was a good thing that I had already decided to purchase him. He went straight into her mouth, and the tag was soon torn off.

Since I was finished with my shopping, we headed for the cash register. There, a lady was arguing with her daughter, who was probably eight or nine years old. They were talking about buying Nanook, the blue-eyed husky.

"Mom, can I get him?" the little girl asked.

"If we do, you aren't going to play with him. He's going on your shelf," was the mother's reply.

"But we had such a hard time finding him!" whined the girl.

"That's why you can't play with him." The mother sounded frustrated, but it was obvious that the girl didn't understand. The toy held a different value for each of them.

The mother happened to glance up to see my daughter chewing on Mystic's horn. Her eyes widened, and I wondered if she was going to ask me if I knew how much he was worth.

It so happens that I didn't, but if I had known then what I know now, nothing would have changed. When your daughter's eyes light up and she laughs aloud, who's going to think about money?

They left, and I paid for my daughter's prize. I walked out of the store, reminded of how priceless joy is.

A perfect collection of Beanie Babies is currently valued at $40,000.

❤ ❤ ❤

I recently sent my niece a Beanie Baby kitten named Flip. Their family owns a real Siamese cat, and while visiting them one time, I saw their cat walk out of the bedroom carrying the stuffed kitten.

# Friends Forever

BY JACQUIE BALODIS

♥ ♥ ♥

Ruth and Kelly had been friends since childhood, but they met under unusual circumstances. Ruth had fallen and received a head fracture that required several brain surgeries when she was seven years old. Kids in her neighborhood teased her because her head had been shaved and she had no hair. She met Kelly in the children's ward of a hospital in Southern California where she was scheduled for another difficult brain surgery.

Kelly was in the hospital because of severe diabetic problems. She also felt the sting of her peers because of seizures caused by her acute diabetes. During their hospital stay the two girls developed a close bond that continued to grow over the years.

Today Kelly is single and lives alone in Saskatchewan, Canada. Ruth lives in San Diego, California, with her husband and children. Although many miles separate their homes, they continued to keep in touch.

A few years ago, Kelly became blind because of her diabetic condition. She had heard people talk about Glory, the Beanie Baby, and she had her heart set on getting the bear for herself. Unfortunately, in Canada Beanie Babies are quite

*Kaitlyn Jensen, age 10*

expensive, and Kelly lives on a limited income. She could not afford the $300 Glory.

Upon hearing of her friend's dilemma, Ruth decided to do her best to buy Glory for Kelly. Since Glory was difficult to locate in the U.S. also, Ruth prayed for help in finding the special little bear. When she finally found one, she couldn't afford it. She was disappointed!

Late one night Ruth was suddenly awakened. She was unable to return to sleep so she turned on the television. At that exact time, a program was offering Glory at a price Ruth could afford. She immediately dialed the number and ordered one for her Canadian friend.

Today Kelly doesn't go anywhere without Glory. The special bear rides in her purse as Kelly and her seeing eye dog take their daily walks or go shopping. Kelly loves to reach into her purse to feel Glory's velvet texture. Whenever she touches her cuddly bear, she remembers her special friend in Southern California.

One avid Beanie Baby fan stood in a long line one morning, trying to add Inch the worm to his collection. While patiently waiting he overheard the lady in front of him place her order: "I'll have two Happy Meals® with worms."

# My Pal Freckles

BY JOAN RAWLINS BIGGAR

❤ ❤ ❤

Freckles, the baby leopard with a pug nose and a puzzled expression, attracted me long before I knew what a Beanie Baby was. After I bought him, I draped him over my car seat where he keeps me company whenever I drive. He's also a big help when I'm trying to locate my car in a parking lot that has a number of vehicles similar to my make and color.

Freckles has repaid me handsomely, not only as a companion and a lost-car locator, but also as an enhancer of human relationships. His cuddly pliability can soothe a cranky grandchild or serve as a conversation starter among adult passengers. His funny little face makes me smile when I feel glum. He builds bridges to strangers—even strangers who zoom past me on the highways.

At a traffic light one day, I glanced over at a car in the next lane. A radio blared from the open windows, and the three occupants spoke loudly in a different language, which intimidated me.

Then the woman in the passenger seat looked my way. The young men with her also stared and grinned. For a

I love my leopard Freckles. He's my best beanie baby.

Madelyn Koehly
age 5½

*Madelyn Koehly, age 5½*

moment I thought she was pointing at me. I gulped. Why was she pointing at me?

"Beanie Baby!" she mouthed, smiling.

I realized that she wasn't pointing at me but at the cuddly leopard beside me. I glanced down at Freckles, then smiled back.

The light turned green. They pulled away. I did, too, feeling a warmth, but also a little ashamed. I knew better than to judge people on first appearances. A floppy critter named Freckles reminded me that deep down inside everyone shares a common trait: we're all kids at heart!

# Dotty, the Missing Dog

### BY PAUL ORT

❤ ❤ ❤

**M**y daughter, Jessica, has a close friend named Dotty. At first glance she doesn't appear like much, but Dotty has taught my family a valuable lesson in faith even though she is only a stuffed Dalmatian.

Jessica took her little toy dog wherever she went. Dotty would sleep with her and eat with her. They would play outside, inside, and anywhere else an active four-year-old might think to take her.

One day we went shopping about thirty miles from our home in Lewistown, Pennsylvania. On the trip home, just past the half-way point, Jessica discovered Dotty was nowhere in sight. We pulled over and searched the car, fearing the worst. Indeed, Dotty was missing. Jessica started to cry.

We turned around and headed back to the store we believed we had left Dotty in. I told Jessica, "It's possible that someone might have picked her up, but we'll try to find Dotty."

My wife, Spring, suggested that they pray about it.

Jessica prayed, "God, please help us find Dotty. Don't let any little kid take her because I love her very much."

Both my wife and I had tears in our eyes as our little girl prayed.

The return trip took what seemed like forever. The entire time I prayed fervently, "Please, God, please don't crush this little girl's faith."

Yet, I told myself that the dog probably wouldn't be there. I steeled myself for the worst.

Jessica soon fell asleep, thumb in her mouth and cheeks streaked with dried tears. We decided to let her sleep so that if Dotty wasn't there we could have time to figure out what to tell her.

When we reached the town, Spring went inside the stores we had shopped in while I stayed in the car with Jessica. Spring didn't find Dotty at the first store, or the second, or the third. Finally she located the spotted dog, lying on the floor in the swimsuit section of the fourth store.

On the way back Spring woke Jessica up by having the dog nuzzle up against her. Jessica gave Dotty a big hug and fell back asleep with a smile on her face.

Later we asked Jessica about the incident, and she replied, "I knew Dotty would be there because God knows she's very important to me."

# Best Friend Bears

BY R. MARK WEBB

**O**ne warm July afternoon in 1995, I was vacationing with my family in Valle Crucis, a small town nestled in the mountains of western North Carolina. We went into a general store to escape the heat and find a cold drink. While wandering through the store, my eight-year-old daughter, Lara, was captivated by two colorful beanbag bears cuddled together on a lonely shelf. The innocent look of love and devotion on their little faces proved impossible to resist. Lara left the store that day with what she called her "Best Friend Bears," one for her and one as a gift for her best friend, Elizabeth.

The Best Friend Bears returned with us to our home in Florida where the heart-shaped tags bearing their names were unwittingly removed. Lara's magenta bear was given the name, Violet, while the teal-colored bear named Wintergreen went home with Elizabeth.

Over the years Elizabeth and Lara's friendship grew through countless slumber parties, church outings, birthday celebrations, and hours of dress-up. The two friends never failed to offer a hug when times were sad or to share a laugh during times of joy.

Though Violet and Wintergreen are beginning to show signs of wear from years of play, the friendship between Lara and Elizabeth has only grown stronger.

With interest in Beanie Babies growing stronger every day, I have recently tried to convince Lara to store Violet in a plastic bag to protect the value of her early edition Beanie Baby. But the money has no meaning to her. After all, how can you put a price on the value of such a friendship?

Someday, the inevitable activities of girls growing into women will distract Lara and Elizabeth. Other interests will prevail, and Violet and Wintergreen will each retire to a box in a closet somewhere. But I believe the real friendship will live on.

Some friendships are meant to last a lifetime.

> To meet the demand the second time around, Ty, Inc. offered twelve styles in 1998, up from ten the year before, in quantities reaching 240 million—enough for every American to have one Happy the hippo, Pinchers the lobster, or Inch the worm.

# Seamore's Story

## BY SHERI KANE

❤ ❤ ❤

My five-year-old son, Andrew, loves to tell stories. He sits for hours drawing pictures and then explains to me the story behind each picture.

During the first Teenie Beanie Babies craze at McDonald's, *The St. Louis Post Dispatch* ran a contest, giving away ten complete Teenie Beanie sets. Entrants had to write a short story about their favorite Teenie Beanies.

Andrew loved *all* of his Beanies and wrote stories about each of them. We entered a few, but he didn't win. His stories were special to me, however. And after he illustrated them, I bound them in a homemade book. We shared his stories with anyone who would listen.

One of his stories was about Seamore the seal who had become very ill. She prayed to God to make her well. (Andrew decided the seal was too pretty to be a boy.) Seamore did everything the doctors told her, but she died anyway. As far as Andrew was concerned, however, the story ended happily. He explained how happy Seamore was to be free of pain and to be with God in heaven.

In August, Andrew's godmother, his precious Aunt GiGi,

was diagnosed with leukemia. Although we prayed for her recovery, she became weaker every day.

One day near Christmas we went to visit her in the hospital. Andrew climbed up on the bed to give her a kiss, and then he handed her Seamore. He curled his legs up on the corner of the bed and told her Seamore's story. There wasn't a dry eye in the room except for Andrew's.

During the next few months, Aunt GiGi kept Seamore by her bed. Frequently we'd notice her stroking the cuddly seal. I took the story Andrew had told her and made it into a poster for her wall.

Aunt GiGi died a few months later. At the funeral, Andrew looked up at me and said "It's okay, Mom. Seamore will show her the way to heaven."

Seamore is a constant reminder of the compassion and love shown by our young son to his precious Aunt GiGi.

In 1996 an event occurred that accelerated interest in purchasing and collecting Beanie Babies: Ty, Inc. officially retired a batch of Beanies and also introduced birthdates and poems on the tags. These poems and birthdates are fun for kids because they like having Beanies that share their birthdate.

# What's on the Menu Today?

## BY LIL HORNE MOTE

♥ ♥ ♥

As a grandmother with interests of my own, I have to admit I was completely unaware of Beanie Babies. However, I do enjoy spending time with my two grandsons, so one day I treated them to lunch at a McDonald's restaurant. Little did I know at the time that McDonald's was offering Teenie Beanies as the current toys in their Happy Meals®.

I entered McDonald's and was amazed at the unusually long lines for the middle of the week. As I stood there waiting, I wondered if I had enough money to purchase two Happy Meals®. *Did the Happy Meals® come with drinks*, I wondered, *or do I have to buy the drinks separately?* I fumbled for my purse to see how much money I had.

A young woman stood in line ahead of me. She was old enough to have children, so I thought I'd take a chance and ask her about the children's meals.

"Pardon me," I said, "are you going to order Happy Meals®?"

"Yes," she said. "I'm buying them for the children I baby sit."

"Do you by any chance know what's in a Happy Meal®?"

"Well," she said, "I think it's seal."

*Seal*? I thought. I stared at her, certain that senility had finally slithered through my brain. "Seal?" I said out loud. Surely they couldn't be offering seal in the kids' meals.

"Yeah," she said. "I already picked up Seamore for my nephew, and now I need to get more for the kids I baby sit."

Suddenly the fog cleared from my brain.

"No, no," I said, "I don't care about the toys. I was just wondering if drinks were included in the price of a Happy Meal®."

# A Gift of Peace

BY ANNETTE TRABUCCO

♥ ♥ ♥

One beautiful spring day I had just parked my car to go to a hair appointment. As I walked along I saw a man who was apparently homeless. He was lying against a wall on the side of a restaurant. I quickly determined what it would cost me for my haircut, then gathered the nerve to walk up to the stranger and ask, "Are you a drinker?"

He smiled and said no.

I believed him because there were no nearby bottles or stench of alcohol. As I looked around, to my surprise and sadness, I saw a young girl with a tangled head of dirty blonde hair sitting between a garbage dumpster and a fast food restaurant building. Apparently both father and daughter had been rummaging through the trash looking for scraps.

I turned and walked over to her. I was overcome with emotion as her beautiful angelic young face looked up at me expectantly. Her eyes expressed hunger and despair as she returned my gaze. Then she quickly looked down.

"I'll be back in a minute," I said. I quickly walked into the fast food restaurant and purchased a bucket of chicken, vegetables, and milk. When I brought the chicken dinner back to the little girl, her father had joined her.

When I handed it to her I realized I had missed my hair appointment, but I didn't care. She thanked me and stood up to give me a kiss on the cheek and a big hug. Then she handed the food to her dad to eat first. Her father only took a little and handed the food and both cartons of milk back to his seven-year-old daughter.

Remembering I had just purchased a few Beanie Babies that were still in the back of

*Kaitlyn Jensen, age 10*

my trunk, I asked if she had any toys. She shook her head.

I smiled to myself thinking about the multi-colored bear, sitting in my trunk just waiting to be loved. I said, "Wait here a few minutes. I'll be right back." Then I hurried to my car and opened my trunk to retrieve Peace. Holding him tightly I said a prayer to God asking Him to keep this little girl safe. I prayed that Peace would bring peace and happiness to her life. I wrote my phone number on the tag as best I could and stuck a quarter in the middle of the tag

I went back with the bear tucked behind my back. I asked the little girl, "Could you do me a big favor?" With a huge smile she nodded.

I brought the bear out from behind my back, and she jumped up! "Could you take care of Peace for me. He needs a friend to love him. My phone number and a quarter are on the tag. You can call me if you ever want to."

She quickly handed her food to her dad and wiped her hands on her sundress. In awe she took Peace in her arms gently and rocked him. I turned to the father and put the remaining money in his pocket and said, "May God bless you both."

As I walked away, I turned back and saw the little girl holding Peace tightly in her arms. I was grateful for the opportunity to share what I had with her and her father.

Though Glory can be purchased in Canada, the Maple Bear is not available for purchase in the U.S.

# God's Perfect Timing

BY BARBARA CURTIS

♥ ♥ ♥

"**O**h look, Sophia!" I exclaimed as we scanned Dr. Bales' selection of prizes. "Beanie Babies!"

My eight-year-old daughter had accumulated thirty wooden nickels from her orthodontist for previous "clean" visits, and she wanted to trade them in for a toy.

Sophia and I studied the bulletin board, listing the prizes available for redeemed wooden nickels. I was elated to see that fifteen wooden nickels could "purchase" one of two new Beanie Babies—Stretch, the ostrich and Rainbow, the chameleon. Though we had close to fifty Beanie Babies floating around our household of eleven kids, I suddenly realized that in the six months since I had last purchased one, many new critters had been released. Despite my pleas, however, Sophia opted for another toy. After all, they were her wooden nickels. She had earned them, not I.

But the "bug" had bitten. The Beanie Baby lust had set in, and I was determined to get one for myself. On the way home, I dashed into several stores that carried the stuffed animals, only to find them sold out. I arrived home empty-handed, but soon forgot my obsession amongst a flurry of diapers and hungry children.

Imagine my surprise when I received a cardboard box in the mail that day—stuffed with Beanie Babies, including Stretch and Rainbow! A woman I had met briefly at a writers' conference five months earlier, a serious Beanie Baby collector, had decided to disperse her collection. Knowing I was a mom who was less interested in collecting and more interested in letting my kids play with their toys, she had mailed us a dozen cuddly critters.

God's perfect timing! Had the Beanie Babies arrived the day before, I never would have known who "really" sent them!

*Patrick Stevens, age 10*

# Mary's Beanie Auction

## BY BRITTANY ALVY (AGE 12)

♥ ♥ ♥

"I'll take the kitten," said Mary.

"You mean the one with the gray stripes?" asked the clerk at the Beanie Barn.

"Yes, that one please."

Mary bought Prance that day, bringing her collection to a total of 176 Beanie Babies. She had collected these little critters for less than a year.

When she returned home she showed her mother her latest Beanie, then put it away.

Back in the kitchen, Mary rummaged around for a snack while her mother prepared dinner.

"So, Mary, you've managed to accumulate a rather large Beanie Baby collection," said her mother.

"Yep, 176. I'm going for 200. That's my goal."

"Don't you think you could use that money for something better?"

"Like what?" Mary couldn't think of anything else she would rather spend her money on.

"You know, like a good cause."

"You mean to help a charity?"

"Sure, why not?"

"You know I would Mom, but I worked hard to earn the money for these Beanies, and I deserve them!"

"I know you do. By the way, Mrs. Galloway called. She has some jobs for you to do this Saturday. Do you have time?"

"Sure! I'm saving up for Princess. I have so many Beanies but not her. It will take me a long time to save up. The Beanie Barn is selling her for $60.00! Do you think you could maybe help me out a bit with $10.00."

"I don't think so, Mary, but I'll tell you what. If you can think of a way to use your Beanie collection for a good cause, I'll buy her for you."

"Okay! You're on!"

The next day Mary set out her entire collection and picked out the ones she no longer wanted. While she was sorting through them she came up with a great plan to use her Beanies for a worthy cause.

"I'll choose sixteen that I don't care if I keep. Starting small is a good start!" she said out loud.

Mary put Mystic, Derby, Happy, Smoochy, Quackers, Zip, Weenie, Dotty, Jolly, Bongo, Hoppity, Seaweed, Mel, Bones, Pinky, and Scoop in a box and sat down at her computer. Before long, she had created flyers announcing her very first Beanie auction.

She walked around the neighborhood with her announcements that read:

---

**COME TO THE BEANIE AUCTION!**

On Saturday Mary Joel is having a Beanie auction.

All the money will go to the Red Cross.

Bring your money or your donations.

Everyone is invited! Drinks will be served!

---

The bright pink flyer caught the attention of one of Mary's friends across the street. As she read the flyer, she remembered that some of her schoolmates collected Beanie Babies, and she decided to make an announcement in class the next day.

Saturday arrived, and a small crowd of twelve people swarmed to Mary's Beanie yard sale. One person even donated her own Beanie Baby for the auction.

When the day was over, Mary had raised over $250 on the auctioned Beanies. She even announced another auction the following week. But the best part of the day wasn't the money, but how it made Mary feel, knowing that she was helping other people. She didn't even care if she got Princess.

After several weeks of auctions, Mary raised over $600 by selling her Beanie Babies. Now she had only twenty Beanies remaining—her favorites!

Finally, Mary announced that her next auction would be her last unless other people wanted to bring their Beanies to sell.

Lo and behold, the following weekend the crowd had doubled and so did the Beanies to be auctioned. Mary told everyone that the auctions would continue as long as people kept coming. But the best news of all was the $1,156.75 that had been raised for the Red Cross! People cheered as they cleared the driveway.

As the crowds dwindled, Mary's mom walked out with a wrapped present in her hand. Mary instantly knew what it was, but stopped her mom before she could give it to her.

"Mom, thanks for getting Princess, but I no longer want her."

"Okay, I can return her. Which one would you like?"

"No, you don't understand. I don't want a Beanie Baby."

"But you worked so hard. How can I reward you?"

"I already got my award, Mom."

"What do you mean."

"Helping people with the money that was raised really made me feel good."

"I'm proud of you, Mary," said her mom.

"The best part of having my collection was when I could share it to help others. I feel a hundred times better auctioning off my Beanies for a good cause than keeping them."

The next day Mary and her mother went down to the Red Cross and donated the money Mary had raised as well as Princess. Smiles a mile wide lit up their faces as they left.

"Well, you wouldn't let me treat you to a new Beanie

Baby for all your hard work," Mary's mother said to her. Then with a smile she asked, 'Would you consider an ice cream sundae instead?"

*Sheri Gonzalez, age 12*

# The Cat Strikes Back

## BY TRISH HOPPER

❤ ❤ ❤

One night, as I tucked my son Timmy into bed, I noticed little lumps rising from under the comforter. Timmy loved to sleep with all the Beanie Babies he owned, and they were everywhere. I smiled as I saw my son buried in the middle of them with some of their cute little faces poking out around him.

As I sat down on the edge of the bed to give him a goodnight kiss I felt what seemed to be an enormous Beanie Baby wriggling beneath me. Suddenly there was this wild meowwwwwwwwwwwwwwwwwwwwww as our poor cat Patches tried desperately to scramble out from under me! He finally wriggled free and bounded under the bed.

Before disappearing completely he glanced back at me with a disgusted expression. Patches had been curled up next to his share of Timmy's Beanie Babies, sleeping quite peacefully until I sat on him.

For days after that fretful event, Patches wouldn't come out from under Timmy's bed except for a quick trip to the litter box. I worried that the poor cat might go hungry.

Then several days later I found my precious Teenie

Beanie, Waddle, put to death! Patches had snuck into my closet and clawed his way through a bag that Waddles was in. Gnawing on him unmercifully, the cat then deposited the Teenie's remains in the litter box!

It must have been Patches' method of revenge. After all, *my* Beanie Baby was the only one he destroyed. None of Timmy's Beanies were touched. As a result, I've learned to be a lot more careful of where I sit.

# All by Himself

BY DIANA L. JAMES

❤ ❤ ❤

Four-year-old Russell was usually a sleepyhead in the morning. But today he bounded out of bed before anyone else in the family was up.

Today was his first day of preschool.

Usually his mom helped him wash his face, brush his teeth, and comb his hair, but this time Russell did it all by himself. When he finished, the sink looked awful! His toothbrush was on the floor, and some of his hair was sticking straight up.

But Russell looked in the mirror and grinned proudly––he had done this *all by himself*.

By the time his older brother and sister reached the breakfast table, Russell had finished his cereal and juice. Plus, he put his dishes in the sink all by himself.

"Your shirt is buttoned wrong," seven-year-old Christina said. She started to fix Russell's buttons.

He pulled away. "I can fix it all by myself," he said with a big smile.

And he did.

The two big kids left to catch their school bus. Dad

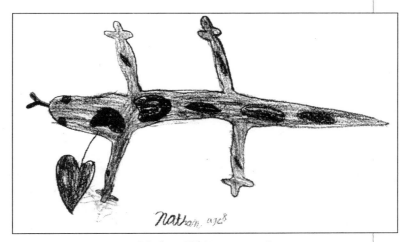

*Nathan Whitman, age 8*

left to go to work, and Mom was busy dressing his baby sister.

Suddenly, Russell felt all alone. He didn't want to go to preschool. He was scared. He wouldn't know anybody there. Maybe nobody would talk to him. Maybe he would be all by himself, without any friends.

"Come on, let's go," said Mom.

Russell panicked. "I'm not going," he said.

Then, suddenly, he had a thought. He rushed to his bedroom and grabbed his favorite Beanie Baby, Lizzy the lizard, off his bed.

"Lizzy's going with me," he said happily. "Lizzy's my buddy. Now I *know* I won't be there all by myself!"

# Say It with a Beanie

## BY JERI CHRYSONG

♥ ♥ ♥

**B**eanie Babies are the "Hallmark Cards" of plush toys. They can be presented to people as gifts "when you care enough to send the very best." For example, when my sister and I returned from a wonderful weekend in Cambria on California's coastline, I sent Seaweed to her as a reminder of the times we spent perched on the rocks, watching one particular silly otter at play.

On another occasion, Patti, the platypus, was given to me before a hospital stay, and she snuggled nicely inside my robe lapel to keep me company. I presented Claude the crab to my teenager, Luc, after a bout with stubborn head butting and the resultant sulking. (Think about it.)

And when my friend, Shelly, bowled three strikes in a row, (four actually), a "turkey" in bowling terminology, I applauded her accomplishment by presenting Gobbles the turkey for her birthday. She, in turn, gave Spunky the cocker spaniel to me as a condolence when Dudley my beloved cocker spaniel died. I fell asleep cradling Spunky in my hands. I can't say whether or not Shelly slept with her turkey.

For almost every occasion, Beanie Babies are the perfect greeting or gift, but their only drawback is they don't fit well in envelopes.

Beanie Babies: "When you care enough to send the very best."

Nortic the Turtle

Nortic the turtle, blue, purple and green
He is nice, not a pinch of mean
He really is different from the rest
But the beanies like him best

By Kimberly Reinhardt

*Kimberly Reinhardt, age 12*

# The Language of Love

BY LINDA EVANS SHEPHERD

♥ ♥ ♥

When my daughter was eighteen months old, we were in a violent car accident. Although Laura had been carefully strapped in her car seat, the force of the crash hurled her onto the freeway. Unfortunately, Laura's injuries were severe. She was left as a brain-damaged quadriplegic on life support.

Laura's daddy, Paul, has been loving and faithful to his daughter all these years. In the beginning, when Laura was in a deep coma, he would sit by her bed and hold her hand. As Laura began to awaken, he continued to hold her hand. But what could Paul say to his beautiful brain-damaged daughter? He longed for a way to connect with her, but communication was difficult because Laura could no longer speak.

The years passed, and Paul continued struggling to find the best way to connect with his twelve-year-old daughter. Finally, his solution came by way of brightly colored Beanie Babies. Recently, when he gave her the latest duck, Jake, and the fat penguin, Waddle, Laura's eyes danced. For a few moments, this little girl and her father did not need words. They spoke the language of love through adorable, plush animals that danced on her pillow and kissed her cheeks.

Now, as Laura's daddy leans down to give her a goodnight kiss, he tucks her in with her latest Beanie Baby. Laura and her dad may speak few words, but with a little help from their cuddly critters, their hearts speak volumes.

When my ten-year-old cousin, Jessica, was six, she was in a car accident that paralyzed her from the neck down. One thing that really makes her happy is Beanie Babies because they are something she can talk about with the other kids at school. She feels just like her peers when she's having fun with kids who love Beanies as much as she does.

Submitted by Emily Bair (age 12)

❤ ❤ ❤

Beanie Babies Righty, Lefty, Libearty, and Britannia are the only Beanies that have never been available in Canada.

# Beanie in Between

BY LYNN D. MORRISSEY

♥ ♥ ♥

I dreaded going home. Though I had been warmly received at my speaking engagement, I wasn't expecting as warm a reception from my daughter, Sheridan. Struggling with the mixed emotions of satisfaction and guilt I hurried through the airport to catch my plane.

Suddenly, I noticed a shop strewn with tantalizing toys for traveling parents still in need of a last minute gift. I took the bait and entered.

Bypassing flashy automatons, I favored a plush pile of crumpled critters. What were these velveteen invertebrates that collapsed in a heap whenever I picked one up and plopped it down?

"Beanie Babies are the rage," the clerk assured. "Your daughter will cuddle the stuffing out of 'em!" Cuddle evoked a wistful longing to scoop Sheridan into my arms as easily as I did this linguini-limp lion. Shelling out my last dollars, I tucked Roary into my purse, hopeful that Sheridan would long for a little cuddling, too.

Later, juggling bags, briefcase, and Beanie Baby, I hurried off the plane. As I approached the gate, Sheridan leaped

My FAVORITE BEaNIe BAby Is RoarY.
RoarY's Whiskers are so cute.
RoarY's eyes are shiney.
Niele
Koehly aGe 6½

*Nicole Koehly, age 6½*

to hug me, then immediately retreated behind her dad. Despite my coaxing, she avoided further hugs and conversation.

It had happened again. Though separated only briefly, Sheridan and I were back to square one. I had worked during part of her early childhood. As a result, we'd gotten off to an awkward start, often with a nanny in-between. Though I was home full-time now, occasional out-of-town conferences reminded Sheridan of my earlier absences.

Although our relationship had improved dramatically and she would always warm up after these halting welcomes, I needed to help her bridge the emotional gap between my departures and arrivals.

On the drive home my husband Michael played chauffeur, and I joined Sheridan in the back seat. I reached for her hand. When she withdrew it, tears sprang to my eyes. Reaching in my purse for a tissue, I fingered a curious lump—Roary!

I set Roary between us on the seat and animated his floppy legs. "Sherrridan," I purred. "My name is Roary. What's yours?"

"Sheridan," she replied. "I'm five, how old are you, Roary?"

"Five, too. Isn't that amazing!" Thus Sheridan conversed with a friend as real to her as any other.

"Do you have a mommy, Roary?"

"Yes, and I love her!"

"I love my mommy, too," she said as she stroked Roary's head. Sheridan intertwined her fingers with mine, as they rested on the cuddly Beanie Baby between us. I knew, in reality, they rested on love.

# Grumpy Grandpa

## BY AMY SANCHEZ

❤ ❤ ❤

**M**y seven-year-old son, Patrick, is an avid collector of Beanie Babies. In fact, our entire family is actively involved in the Beanie search.

One day, which happened to be the third anniversary of my father-in-law's death, our family went shopping at the mall. As we walked around we talked of the fond memories of the man we affectionately referred to as "Grumpy Grandpa." As always, we stopped at a toy store to see if they had any Beanie Babies.

While there, the clerk explained they were offering a promotion whereby every one hundredth paying customer would receive one of the two new Beanie Baby holiday bears.

"And," she said, "we haven't given away any bears yet."

My husband handed Patrick a dollar in order to make a small purchase. Maybe he would be the lucky winner.

My baby daughter had started to fuss so I took the stroller into the mall to walk her around. I window-shopped for awhile but kept looking around for my son and husband.

They seemed to be taking a long time to purchase a dollar toy so I went back in the store to check on them.

Sure enough, Patrick was a one hundredth paying customer and won Halo, the Angel bear!

When we returned to our van, I took Halo out of the bag. I was amazed to find that Halo's birthday is August 31st, the same day as Grumpy Grandpa's birthday! I read the poem from Halo's tag.

It said that Halo was like a guardian angel, and there was no need to be afraid when going to sleep because Halo would always be there to watch over us.

Our family was quite touched by this remarkable coincidence. Patrick will always remember the day he won Halo, the Beanie that was born the same day as Grandpa. There is no way we will ever part with this adorable Beanie who seemed to hand-deliver us a message from Grumpy Grandpa in heaven. We sure do miss him, but we're comforted to know that he got his wings!

# Little Lost Dog

BY JESSICA POWELL

It had been a long day, filled with the Beanie craze, when I took a walk around our shop to restore some order to the Beanie Babies. On the corner of a shelf, a dirty white dog looked sadly misplaced. It was covered in black spots that drew attention away from its beat-up, chipped eyes and mangled fur.

The creature's haphazard appearance confessed the story of childhood love. Still attached was the heart-shaped tag, feebly proclaiming that his name was Spot, one of the original Beanies. I was touched to see that one of these small toys was being loved in such a way. Yet, I had absolutely no idea where he'd come from or how to return him to his young owner.

I placed him on a shelf above our regular Beanies with the hope that this lost Beanie's owner would soon be found. Over the next couple of weeks, people expressed great interest in Spot because he was still of great value despite his mangled condition. I told them that he wasn't mine to sell.

As weeks passed, Spot looked more and more lonely on that empty shelf. We began to give up hope of seeing him reunited with the loving child, who accidentally left him in our care.

One afternoon, a woman came in to inquire about where she might buy a zebra Beanie Baby because her young daughter had lost hers. After a lengthy conversation about checking places like Beanie fairs, she added, "Yeah, she lost Ziggy and Spot."

At first, I thought I hadn't heard her correctly. The words occurred as an afterthought, with the smallest breath and no hope. But it gave me shivers and I asked, "Spot?"

She answered in a quiet voice, "Yeah, she lost Spot."

As her voice trailed off, it all started to make sense. In my exhilaration, I somehow managed to grab hold of the small dog and blurt out the words, "Not this Spot?"

Immediately, I knew we'd found Spot's owner. Her face lit up and she cried, "You found Spot!" She explained that her young daughter had searched everywhere for this beloved dog that was her favorite. "It was heartbreaking. Spot's her favorite Beanie, and we've looked everywhere."

She continued, "Every night before going to bed, my daughter prays, 'Dear God, if I never find Spot, would you please make sure he's in a safe place and that someone loves him?' Then she cries herself to sleep."

My eyes filled with tears as I watched the woman bolt from our store in her excitement to get home with her precious cargo.

# Angel to the Rescue

## BY LYNN O'BRIEN

💜 💜 💜

This past summer my son needed an operation on his right eye to repair a damaged muscle. I asked him what he would like for a present when he came out of surgery.

He replied, "Mom, I want one of the 'new' Beanie Babies-Rocket, Kuku, or Whisper."

Knowing they had just been released, I started searching for one a few weeks in advance. I drove around the better part of Vermont, but to no avail. Either the Beanies couldn't be found, or the people who had them were charging as much as $30 apiece since they had just been placed on the market. These Beanies were considered a "hot" item at the time.

As a last ditch effort, I decided to place an ad in the *Ty Guestbook*, hoping somebody might come to my aide. I explained the situation regarding my son's upcoming surgery and asked if anyone could help me.

My ad was answered by an "angel" in New Jersey named Sue. Not only did she offer to mail my son the Beanie Baby named Rocket, but she also sold it to me at cost. Plus, she didn't even wait until I sent her the money!

Rocket

Jessica Freitas

*Jessica Freitas, age 7*

She mailed out Rocket the very day I contacted her, and it arrived in time for my son's operation. It put such a smile on his face when he came out of recovery and saw his brand new Beanie Baby!

Sue and I have stayed in touch since then. It is so heart-warming to know that there are generous people in the world. Not everybody is into Beanie Babies to make money. Sue was an angel to help us in our time of need, and we will never forget her kindness to our family.

# The Lap Cat

BY SUSAN TITUS OSBORN

♥ ♥ ♥

**M**y mother loves to shop, and even after my two boys were grown, she could still shop circles around me. She would browse in almost every store in the mall. But that all changed one fateful August morning in 1993 when she suffered a massive brain hemorrhage. Her planned schedule of luncheons, bridge foursomes, painting lessons, and beauty salon appointments was canceled—forever.

Today she lives in a nursing home in Scottsdale, Arizona, and because of the stroke, she is paralyzed on her right side. She hasn't regained the ability to speak in spite of continued therapy, although she can say a few words. Her communication is limited to facial expressions. Through these she makes known her thoughts, smiling or frowning, about what is being said or done. We've learned to keep our conversations short and light-hearted when visiting her.

My husband Dick and I have also learned how to transport Mother in our rental car, so we're able to take her out to lunch when we visit. We continue to frequent the Chinese, Mexican, and seafood restaurants that were favorites before her stroke. Weather permitting, we can take her sightseeing in the park, to museums, or to art galleries.

As we push her through the halls of her new home, we are constantly stopping so she can greet the other residents with a smile or a squeeze of her left hand. Several of the staff have admitted she is one of their favorite residents.

Her world has shrunk, but she is content. Once she was a wealthy woman with many worldly possessions. Now material things don't seem to matter to her anymore.

When I visit her, I usually take a gift. Once I asked if she wanted some flowers. She shook her head no. She hadn't eaten the last box of chocolates I took, so I was looking for new ideas.

Then while shopping one day I saw a shelf of Beanie Babies. Snip gazed at me with big blue eyes, and I remembered a cat my mother once owned that looked just like Snip. I quickly purchased the cute little bundle of fur and took it to Arizona on my next visit.

When I placed Snip on Mother's lap, she stroked the cat's fur as if it were real. When she looked up at me she beamed an enormous smile, and I knew I had found the perfect gift.

I love my leopard Freckles. He's my best Beanie Baby.

Submitted by Madelyn Koehly (age 5)

# Things to Do:
# How to Make a Beanie Baby Ark

## BY ELLEN BERGH

**Y**our Beanie Babies will love their ark, where they can peek out their porthole windows to watch the world.

Supplies needed:

- ♥ Three large pieces of poster board (24" x 36")
- ♥ Cardboard shoe holder for nine pairs of shoes
- ♥ One package shake shingles for roof (optional)
- ♥ Cardboard box larger than shoe holder to float ark on.
- ♥ Compass or soup can to trace portholes
- ♥ Contact paper, crayons, pencil, stickers, or poster paint

1. Select a shoe holder for nine pairs of shoes (13x27), so that you have nine staterooms for your Beanie Baby passengers. Assemble shoe holder, place poster board right side down, set shoe holder on top of wrong side and trace the

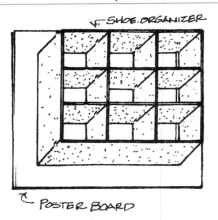

rectangular openings—these will become the Beanies' state-rooms.

2. Remove shoe holder and draw a circle in the middle of each rectangle for the portholes. These will be just big enough for your Beanie Babies to stick their heads out. Use a compass or can to trace the circles.

3. Have an adult cut the circles with a knife and trim the poster board to the size of the box.

4. Decide how you want your ark to look. You could color around the portholes, or cover with contact paper and cut out circles.

5. Set this box with the portholes in it on top of a larger box. Poster board glued to the lower deck of the ark may be painted. You can even add waves.

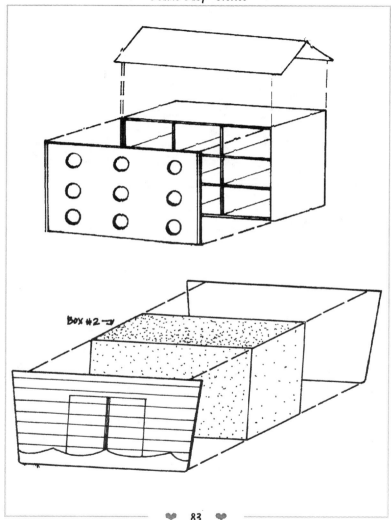

BOX #2 →

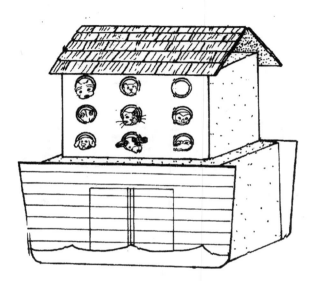

6. The third piece of poster board is the roof of your ark. Using a yardstick, draw a line down the middle of the entire length of the poster board and carefully fold it in half, so it looks like a tent. You can glue shingles made for dollhouses onto the roof, or use noodles that are spray painted. No matter what you decide, your Beanie Baby passengers will be thrilled to be on board their very own ark.

HAPPY SAILING!

# Special Delivery

## BY SANDRA JENSEN

♥ ♥ ♥

My ten-year-old daughter Kaitlyn loves cats. As a result, our family has six of them. Three are all white, and though no one else can tell them apart, Kaitlyn knows Vanilla from Whitey and Whitey from Blondie.

Kaitlyn also loves to get mail. She hurries out to the end of the driveway whenever she sees the mail truck coming down the street and waits patiently for the postal carrier to drive up to our mailbox. Though Kaitlyn doesn't usually receive cards or invitations by mail, she is content with an occasional magazine or toy catalog. As a result of her daily outings to the mailbox, Kaitlyn has developed a fond relationship with Rosie, our postal carrier.

It didn't take long for Kaitlyn to discover that Rosie also loves cats. One day when Kaitlyn received a cat calendar in the mail from her grandmother, Rosie and Kaitlyn oohed and aahed over the cute little kittens splashed across the twelve-month calendar.

After that, Rosie would often share with Kaitlyn some of the adventures she had with her own two Siamese cats named Fred and Ethel. Sometimes Kaitlyn would even carry one of her own cats to the end of the driveway to show it off to Rosie. Following these late afternoon chats, Kaitlyn always skipped into the house and chirped out the latest news from our mail lady.

So I knew something was wrong the day Kaitlyn walked quietly into the kitchen and set the mail on the counter.

"Something the matter?" I asked.

"Ethel's dead," she said with a sigh. She picked up Jericho, our butterscotch-colored tabby, and caressed him lovingly.

"Who's dead?" I asked.

"Ethel. Rosie's cat Ethel. She ran out of the house and was run over by a car."

"Oh, how awful," I said.

"Rosie took her to a vet, but she still died. Rosie's really sad. She says Fred walks around the house and cries because he misses Ethel so much, and that makes Rosie cry, too."

"I'm sorry, Kaitlyn," I said, putting my arms around her. "It's hard to lose a friend."

Kaitlyn nodded, then slowly shuffled off with Jericho still in her arms.

Several minutes later Kaitlyn reappeared.

"Mom, I have an idea. How about if I give my Beanie Baby Snip to Rosie? She looks just like Ethel. I could leave it in the mailbox for her."

"That's really nice," I said. "Put the red flag up so Rosie will know there's something inside."

Rosie was thrilled when she discovered the cuddly Siamese in the mailbox. "Oh, Kaitlyn, this cat looks just like Ethel," she said.

From the moment Rosie discovered little Snip waiting for her in the mailbox, she has kept the cuddly blue-eyed Siamese right beside her in her mail truck.

Rosie eventually did get another Siamese cat as a companion for Fred, but she didn't name the new cat Ethel. Instead, she named her Kaitlyn.

*Patrick Stevens, age 10*

# Glow-in-the-Dark Beanie

## BY NICOLE SKROCKI

❤ ❤ ❤

**M**y daughter Brooke loved Beanie Babies and had gathered quite a collection. She had around fifteen and loved them all. But her favorite was Lefty, the democratic donkey. Lefty now sits on my dresser next to a picture of my daughter. Brooke had to undergo several radiation treatments for a tumor, and the only way she would enter the radiation room was to have Lefty by her side.

One time, when little Lefty was inadvertently left behind, my husband had to walk back to the hotel room where we had been staying to retrieve him. My husband arrived back just in time, and Brooke bravely entered the radiation room with Lefty tucked under her arm.

Brooke died of Wilms' tumor in September of 1997, and her sister now continues the Beanie Baby collection in memory of her. Needless to say, Lefty probably consists of plastic pellets that glow-in-the-dark, but he is priceless to us. You see, without him Brooke might not have managed the difficult radiation treatments that bought her—and us—an extra six months. Six precious months that we will never forget.

# The Bear of Great Worth

## BY JULIA SCHUCHARD (AGE 11)

❤ ❤ ❤

It was the first day of our family trip, and I couldn't decide what to spend my allowance on. Should I buy a Snoopy key chain in the cartoon store? A T-shirt in the Minnesota store? Or maybe a ride on the roller coaster? With hundreds of stores to choose from, our stop at the Mall of America was definitely a place I could "shop till I dropped."

Then I saw him in the toy store window. A small, colorful bear sat on a shelf all by himself. It was the most beautiful Beanie Baby I had ever seen. I checked the tag—Garcia, $70. I pulled my money from my pocket. All I had was a crumpled $10 bill. *Not even close*, I thought sadly. I put Garcia back and decided on a purple souvenir pen instead.

As we drove to our cabin for a week of fishing in Northern Minnesota, I couldn't get Garcia out of my mind. Images of his button-black eyes and fur the color of spring whirled in my head. I wondered if I'd ever see him again.

Time passed quickly. I swam in the lake, fed the ducklings, and caught my first fish. But one day it rained so hard my parents took my brother and me into town to pick up groceries. As I walked along the nearly-deserted streets, a sign in a small gift shop caught my eye: "Beanie Babies here."

I pushed open the heavy glass door and looked around. I saw candles, clay necklaces, and stained-glass lamps. But over in a corner stood a wood basket filled with Beanie Babies. Maybe I could find Chip to add to my cat collection.

As I sorted through the stuffed animals, I suddenly stopped. There on the bottom of the basket I recognized a tie-dyed bear. Why was Garcia mixed in with all the others? He should be behind the counter with the more expensive Beanies.

I was afraid to look at the price tag, but I finally reached in and held my breath—five dollars. I couldn't believe it. Garcia was finally mine! I held him close and handed the salesclerk my money. As I walked away I overheard my mom tell another shopper, "Did you know that bear is worth a lot?"

"He sure is!" I smiled and hugged Garcia tightly.

My favorite Beanie Baby is Mystic the unicorn. I always love to get Beanie Babies because I love to play with them. They are so cute and cuddly.
Submitted by Julie Licata

# Peace

## BY CATHY HAMILTON

💜 💜 💜

As a child of the sixties, I have always been a true believer in peace. Everyone I knew back then liked to flash each other the peace sign. I'll never forget how someone once mowed the distinctive round symbol into a large lawn in a nearby town. Whenever I drive past that area I always think back thirty years to when people really believed in the concept of peace.

So when Ty, Inc. came out with a bear named Peace, I knew I had to have it. I stood in front of a store one cold morning, the long line snaking around the corner of the shop, hoping to be one of the lucky ones to snag Peace. Wouldn't you know it! There were sixty-two bears, and my number was sixty-three! But for some reason I stayed in line. When I finally neared the front door my heart was pounding. I wanted that little stuffed animal so bad, but to this day I still don't know how I got one.

Thrilled to be holding my very own Peace bear in my hands, I looked it over, then read the swing tag. Suddenly a cold chill ran through my body, and I was back again with my brother Curtis. You see, Peace's birthdate is February 1, which was also my brother's birthday. Curtis was killed in Vietnam in 1969, and the very last thing I ever saw him do was flash me the peace sign from the airplane just before it took off to take him to the other side of the world.

Eventually I was able to purchase several Peace bears for my two sisters and my mom. Somehow knowing that Peace and Curtis were born on the same day, and that Curtis sacrificed his life in order to maintain peace, has made everyone in our family rest a little easier.

by Sheri Gonzalez

*Sheri Gonzalez, age 12*

# Poor Nanook

## BY NANCY SEBASTIAN MEYER

❤ ❤ ❤

The big yellow bus screeched to a halt in front of me. The doors folded open. I smiled at the bus driver, as my seven year old made her way to the front of the bus and down the stairs. She jumped from the last step into my arms and hung on tightly.

I kept one arm wrapped around Becky as we walked carefully around the front of the bus and crossed the street. The bus rumbled past us and was soon out of sight. Immediately Becky burst into tears! They didn't seem like the "I'm tired" kind of tears, or the "somebody was mean to me" tears. She was literally sobbing, and I knew I'd have to settle her down before I would be able to understand a word she said.

"Are you hurt, honey?" I asked. Seeing her shake her head, I continued, "Was someone mean to you?" Again her head went back and forth. "Did something happen at school?"

This time she nodded her head vigorously and shakily whispered, "Nanook."

Trying to get a handle on the situation, I asked, "Did you lose Nanook?"

Tears welled up in her eyes again. "No," she whispered. She dug the little dog out of his safe spot in her backpack. The next words were dredged from her very soul. "I lost his tag!" Clasping him tightly, she sobbed, "He'll never be the same. Poor Nanook."

I held her close, with Nanook sandwiched between us. I whispered in her ear, "We can get a new Nanook with a tag, and then this Nanook will be especially yours."

Becky held very still for several moments thinking about my words. Then she lifted a radiant face to mine and said, "That's a great idea, Mom." She looked at little Nanook. "You are my most special Beanie, and you're all mine."

Dear Mrs. Osborn and Mrs. Jensen:

I love my cute and cuddly Beanies. One of my favorite Beanie Babies is KuKu, the white bird with pink hair. He's my newest Beanie Baby. I always like my newest Beanie best. But Nanook is still my all time favorite.

Becky Meyer (age 7)

# Love Wrapped in Fur

BY RICHARD PARKER

♥ ♥ ♥

Each year since 1991 our church has taken a trip to Rochester, New York, to work with children at a place called "The Pines of Perinton." For an entire week we tell the children stories, do crafts, serve refreshments, and play games. Each year on Friday before we return to Alabama we give each child a special surprise.

When we returned home in July 1997 we decided we would give the children Beanie Babies at the end of our 1998 trip. For twelve months we bought and traded in order to accumulate the one hundred Beanie Babies we would need for the children. Retirement announcements were great because we could trade retired Beanies for two or sometimes three regular ones. By the end of June we had 107 Beanie Babies.

During the entire week at The Pines, we could hardly wait to give the children the special gifts we had for them. When Friday finally came we put each Beanie Baby in a paper bag to hand out at the conclusion of a pizza supper.

Giggles and shouts of joy filled the air when the children started opening the bags. The smiles on their faces told the whole story.

by: Sheri Gonzalez

*Sheri Gonzalez, age 12*

For us a Beanie Baby was a simple expression of affection, but for the children at the Pines of Perinton it was love wrapped up in the faces of Chip, Roary, Sly, Wrinkles, and all their Beanie friends.

# The Smile of a Child

BY MARNIE KNIGHT

❤ ❤ ❤

Being a Beanie Baby fanatic, I once waited patiently outside a store for many hours in order to purchase Glory, Fortune, Rocket, and Wise. These four Beanies would complete my collection. However, I do like to keep a couple extra Beanie Babies for trading purposes, so I'm never opposed to picking up whatever Beanie I can find.

While I was standing in line, I noticed a girl around eleven or twelve who had been waiting nearly as long as I had. Since I had shopped at this store before, I was familiar with their habit of waiting until there was no one in their store, at which time they would bring out new and retired Beanies. So I came back later in the day and patiently waited until a few minutes after the last customer left the store before entering. When I walked in, the little girl, who had been there earlier, followed behind me.

As I wandered around the shelves containing the Beanie Babies, I quickly found GiGi, Fetch, Ants, and Early. Without hesitation I scooped them up and was about to hurry over to the cashier when I noticed the young girl who had followed me into the store. There were big tears rolling down her face as she looked around the display for any new or retired Beanies I might have overlooked. We had both narrowly missed getting Glory earlier that day, and I could tell she was really upset.

I leaned over and whispered to her, "Do you have this one," as I held up GiGi. She shook her head while her face remained downcast.

"Here. I want you to have GiGi," I said as I handed it to her. Several times I asked her the same question about Fetch, Ants, and Early until she had all four of the Beanie Babies I had found. By the fourth Beanie she wore a radiant smile on her face and jumped up and down yelling thank you, thank you, thank you! Even the staff came by to say thank you.

After all the serious collecting and investing that has become a major component of the Beanie Baby trade, it takes the smile of a child to remind us why Beanie Babies were first created!

First Mistake: "Beanie" was misspelled on the sewn-in tag of Libearty Bear (Libearty is intentionally misspelled to include the word "bear"). "Beanie" appeared as "Beanine." Libearty Bear with its erroneous tag is now a collector's item.

# Hooked

BY MARY JO HOCH

♥ ♥ ♥

I never meant to get "hooked." Actually, I inadvertently started collecting Beanie Babies because I belong to a fan club called "PEACE." Of course, when I found out there was a Beanie Baby named Peace, I knew I had to have it. And, naturally, I fell in love with it.

A short time later I was shopping and spied Baldy, the Beanie Baby eagle. Well, my husband is bald, and he loves eagles, so I bought Baldy. Shortly after that, I discovered Blackie. My dad always called me Blackie when I was a little girl, so I added the black circus bear to my growing menagerie.

Before long, my collection had grown to 105 Beanie Babies and twelve Teenie Beanies. Little did I know when I first started purchasing these cuddly critters, how much therapeutic value they would have for me.

Due to multiple sclerosis I am frequently confined to my home. There is one room in our house that is my "sanctuary," but these days we call it the Beanie Baby room. On days when I feel blue I look around at all my "babies" and they make me smile.

I am really thankful for my Beanie Babies, and I hope that Ty Warner and his staff know how much joy they bring to so many people.

*Devan Lyng, age 7*

# Spreading Cheer

## BY SANDRA JENSEN

♥ ♥ ♥

"What can I get you, Aunt Elva?" I always asked my aunt when I visited her in the retirement home.

"Nothing, dear, nothing," she would answer absently. After Uncle Gordon died, she seemed to have lost her zest for life.

I looked around at all the other residents in the center. Elva's roommate was bedridden from a stroke, while other people pushed walkers or lined up in wheelchairs by the nurse's station for a little human contact. They all needed a smile and someone to visit with them.

One day, while my ten-year-old daughter, Kaitlyn, and I were shopping, she pulled me over to a display rack recently filled with a new shipment of Beanie Babies. I marveled at the colorful variety of little critters and found myself picking out four. With several nieces and nephews, I rationalized, they would make great gifts.

A few days later we were getting ready to visit Aunt Elva. Struggling to think of something to bring her, I quickly remembered the Beanie Babies sitting in my room.

"Kaitlyn, grab the bag with the Beanies," I yelled as we hurried out the door.

After we visited a while, we handed Aunt Elva Spunky, the honey-colored cocker spaniel, because she once had a dog. The moment she pulled the Beanie out of the bag, she smiled and stroked the dog's soft fur.

"How sweet," she said, holding it up for her roommate, Shirley, to see. "Now I have my own little dog to keep me company—Pretty," Shirley said with a crooked smile as she lay in her bed straining to see. In all the times I had come to visit my aunt, I had never heard Shirley speak before today.

"Mom," Kaitlyn said as she pulled me over to whisper in my ear. "Let's give one to Shirley. She needs a friend, too." I nodded, and Kaitlyn pulled out Doby and gave it to Shirley. Kaitlyn took the cuddly dog and put it up to Shirley's face, rubbing its soft fur against her cheek.

"Ooooh," she said, and though she struggled with words we couldn't understand, the expression on her face said it all. Elva and Shirley held up their two dogs, admiring them like children delighted with their new toys.

"You know, Kaitlyn, I can always pick up more Beanie Babies. Why don't we ask the nurse who else might need a little cheering up."

"Mrs. Skinner could definitely use a little cheer," nurse Robin explained while we stood at the nurses' station.

"Do you like cats?" I asked Mrs. Skinner as I approached her with my sack of Beanie Babies. I do believe she thought I had a real kitten in the bag and was about to give her one, so she vehemently shook her head no.

"Then how about a kangaroo," I said as I pulled out Pouch. Relieved it wasn't a kitten, Mrs. Skinner reached for the momma kangaroo with its baby in its pouch and giggled like a schoolgirl.

"Mr. O'Dell used to have a cat. He'd probably like Snip," the nurse suggested upon overhearing our conversation. When we passed Mr. O'Dell's room he was asleep so we put the Siamese cat right in front of him on his bedside tray.

Later when we said our good-byes and left, we passed Mr. O'Dell's room on the way out. He was wide awake, and little Snip sat on his pillow right beside him. A large grin lit up his face, and we waved to him as we walked by.

"Let's do this again," Kaitlyn said as we left the center. I smiled and put my arm around her.

The next day we stopped at a local gift shop to purchase four more cuddly companions. We were all set for our next visit with Aunt Elva and the folks at the retirement center.

> Notable Quote: "My Beanie Babies are being held hostage." (Retailer referring to the UPS strike)

# Derby to the Rescue

BY STEPHANIE E. SEIPP

*It's time for a horse*, I remember thinking to myself as I looked into the barn that came with our new house. We finally had bought our dream house, and it came complete with a fenced corral and barn. It seemed as if everyone had a horse in this neighborhood, and during the cooler hours of summer, I often observed these beautiful animals prancing around the fields and trails.

As I turned to go into the house, I waved to my next door neighbor, who was out feeding her horses. Lori had recently moved in with her parents, bringing along her two-year-old daughter Leah, as well as Champ and Nimby, two beautiful paint horses. I learned a lot about horses while watching Lori, and she had offered to help me find my "dream horse" when I was ready.

Well, I was more than ready. Owning a horse had always been a childhood dream.

Later that afternoon my husband said to me, "I'm sorry, honey, but the timing just isn't right for the expense of a horse right now."

Deep down I knew he was right. I tried to put the disappointment behind me, but when I entered a gift shop to purchase a birthday present for my daughter, I spotted Derby, a cuddly brown Beanie Baby horse with a black mane. He had a smile from ear to ear that cheered me up immediately, and he was the last one left. I decided to buy him and resolved then and there that he would keep me company until the real thing came along.

I knocked on Lori's door later to show off my "new horse," and two-year-old Leah opened her arms wide to welcome Derby with a big hug. When it became obvious how attached she was to him, I left him there to keep her company.

A few weeks later, Lori commented that Leah carried her new pal everywhere, squeezed under her arm wherever she went. Lori was especially grateful that Leah had this lovable companion because of the wrenching separation they had all experienced when Lori and her husband had divorced. Of course, I never had the heart to ask for Derby back, and it just wouldn't have been the same to buy a new one.

But I am content to wait for my dream horse. This experience made me realize that God uses different means to provide comfort to people, and this time the comfort came in the shape of a cuddly critter named Derby.

# Doby, My Computer Mentor

BY SUSAN TITUS OSBORN

❤ ❤ ❤

Some of us born in the first half of this century struggle with our computers. We are dependent upon our children and grandchildren to teach us which buttons to push and what to do with our mouse.

Being in this category, and being an author, has created a dilemma. I've had to develop computer skills to make a living. However, I do not consider my computer warm and friendly—at least I didn't until a couple of months ago.

My husband and I were browsing in a store, waiting for our name to be called at the restaurant next door, when I was drawn to an enormous box overflowing with fuzzy lovable creatures. I reached in and pulled out a black and brown dog named Doby that resembles my own dog, Kavic. I couldn't resist.

Now when my computer screen beeps at me and flashes the message, "You have performed an illegal operation," I don't despair. I just look at my new found friend, perched on top of my hard drive. Doby smiles down at me and encourages me. I have learned that when all else fails I should turn the blasted contraption off and start all over again.

# Smiling on the Inside

BY R. MARK WEBB

**R**eluctantly, I agreed to drive my youngest daughter, Lara, to a local McDonald's in search of a Teenie Beanie Baby. This quest was not high on my list of desirable things to do on a Saturday afternoon.

But moments earlier, a telephone call from a friend renewed Lara's hope in finding one of the cuddly creatures that so far had eluded her capture. Mom had conveniently made a run for the grocery store, so Daddy's duty was calling.

It was not an enviable task. I had already tasted the insanity of this craze a week earlier when I innocently stopped at a McDonald's for lunch on the same day the first "Teenies" were introduced. After getting my food approximately twenty minutes later, I promised myself to avoid such a mistake again. However, surrounded by a family of Beanie Baby lovers, I should have known my pledge never had a chance.

Arriving at the restaurant, we waded through the crowd and waited patiently in line to complete our mission. Some time later we triumphantly carried five Happy Meals® with

*Eric Brooks, age 8*

us to a booth. Of course, Lara wasn't hungry, leaving me with five bags of food now void of their coveted prizes.

As I sat across from my daughter, pondering the lengths to which we might go to satisfy this craving for Beanie Babies, I came to a significant conclusion: I was eating way too many hamburgers. But in a sincere attempt to understand this mania, I asked, "Why do you love Beanie Babies so much?"

With a look of surprise that someone could be so ignorant as to ask such a silly question, Lara pondered her reply. Then she simply answered, "Because they make me smile on the inside."

As she resumed her inspection of the new treasures, I was struck by a sudden flash of insight. Through the words of my daughter I was reminded that true joy is found in the simple and sometimes seemingly insignificant things in life.

How often do we miss the joy found in giving or receiving a kind word, a friendly smile, a small act of kindness? Before me I saw the delight a tiny Teenie Beanie could bring reflected in the brightness of my little girl's eyes.

As we left McDonald's that afternoon, I knew I had eaten too many hamburgers. But I was smiling on the inside, too.

# Grandma's Beanie Stories

BY ROSALIE CAMPBELL

♥ ♥ ♥

"**G**randma, Grandma," shrieked four-year-old Christian, as he ran into his grandmother's house for a visit. "Do you have any new Beanie Babies?"

With a twinkle in her eye, Jeanette replied, "Let's go check the cabinet in my bedroom."

The eager youngster took his grandmother's hand and dashed up the stairs in search of the newest face among her collection of Beanies. Dozens of colorful creatures lined the shelf of the cabinet. Christian scrutinized all the animals through the glass door. His brown eyes widened as he exclaimed, "I see it! It's a lion!"

Opening the door, Jeanette reached in and picked up the Beanie Baby with the yellow mane. She looked at the attached tag and reported, "His name is Roary."

"Oh! Please, tell me a story about Roary," Christian pleaded.

The two settled into a nearby cozy chair. Jeanette loved these special times with her grandson, since it gave her an opportunity to share the Beanies as well as teach Christian about Bible characters.

While Christian held Roary, his grandmother told him about a courageous shepherd boy named David who guarded his sheep at night. Lions hid in the dark valleys and preyed on the weak and timid sheep if the shepherd was not around to protect them.

Jeanette explained, "We are like sheep, Christian. We are easily frightened when danger is near. God is our Good Shepherd. He loves us and takes care of us just like when David kept his sheep from the lions' ferocious attacks."

Christian nodded his head. "I remember when you told me about the whale named Orca," he commented. "I bet Jonah was scared, too."

"I'm sure he was," agreed Jeanette. "Do you remember what happened in that story?"

"Yes, Grandma," he replied excitedly. "God make that whale spit Jonah right out of his tummy so he wouldn't have to stay in all that yucky stuff."

Jeanette laughed. How she treasured these special times with her young grandson.

> The Internet is largely responsible for the craze surrounding the stuffed critters.

# Santa Beanie

## BY MARK SOCKWELL

❤ ❤ ❤

I was surfing the Internet in November 1997 and came across a Web site called "Santa Beanie"(put together by Brad Gilchrist, one of the creators of the comic strip "Nancy"). It intrigued me so I visited the site. To my surprise, they were asking for Beanie Baby donations for children's hospitals.

I thought it was a wonderful idea so I decided to do something similar for the needy and underprivileged in my area. Using a Web site that I often frequent, I launched a plea to my fellow Web mates to participate in a special "Santa Beanie Project." The purpose of this project was to help deprived children have a brighter Christmas and to show them that people around the world do care.

As the project unfolded, I thought it would be an interesting challenge to see how many people from different states would become involved. People really responded. Over sixty packages arrived from around the United States. Some people donated Beanie Babies in the name of a loved one. A group of kindergarten children from Lawrenceville, Virginia, who are themselves underprivileged, sent me ten

Beanie Babies for this project. A military family, stationed in Okinawa, Japan, even donated a Beanie Baby. Another lady donated one on behalf of her son stationed in Korea.

In all, over 165 Beanie Babies were donated. There were just enough so that I was able to give one Beanie Baby to each of the 165 disadvantaged kids from my local area in Cumberland County, New Jersey, who attended a special Christmas Party on December 21, 1997, sponsored by a local country club.

*Taylor Osborn, age 7*

This was one of the most heartwarming and rewarding charity projects I've ever been involved in. I was overwhelmed with the generosity and support by total strangers from around the world. What amazes me is that this project became a reality in just three short weeks. And it was all made possible by the combined efforts of modern technology and compassionate people.

# An Online Romance

BY VICKY GEISMAN

♥ ♥ ♥

I am a forty-four-year-old grandmother who recently became a mother. I officially adopted my four-year-old
grandson in March of 1998 even though I have taken care
of him since he was nine days old. He was born with a rare
form of leukemia and an even rarer form of Down's Syn-
drome.

Though I don't have a lot of spare time since becoming a
mom again, I do occasionally go into a chat room on the
Internet. During one of these "chat" sessions, I mentioned
that one of my hobbies was collecting Beanie Babies. A
gentleman in Arizona, intrigued by my description of the
stuffed animals, began chatting back. During our conversations, I explained to him the "finer points" of collecting
Beanies.

From that point on, we began a friendly online relationship. As we chatted via the Internet, I also explained to
him about my grandson and how I originally collected the
Beanie Babies in order to decorate his room.

Over a period of months, our online relationship grew.
We soon spent hours together via e-mail, on the telephone,

and zipping tons of snail mail back and forth across the country. We were in love! In fact, my beau even asked me to marry him online. Six weeks later he flew to Oklahoma. He packed up my grandson and me and moved us back to Arizona to be with him.

We are now happily married, and my new husband and grandson are the best of buddies. The three of us are a family, and we especially enjoy going on Beanie Baby safaris together. And to think that a six-dollar Beanie Baby and the Internet brought us together.

*Aaron Rucker, age 8*

# Spot, the Safety Dog

## BY KAREN H. WHITING

❤ ❤ ❤

I gazed out the open front door at Becky's car, filled to the brim with most of her worldly possessions. My oldest daughter was leaving home to begin her first teaching job. I stood in the entry, holding hands with her and with my younger daughter, Darlene. We were praying before their departure. I felt my heart beat rapidly as we finished. Darlene would go along to help with the driving and moving.

Just as they walked out the door, Daniel, my eight-year-old son, came bounding down the stairs yelling, "Wait! You can't go yet."

"Why not?" Becky asked.

"I want you to take Spot with you," he replied as he held out his Beanie Baby dog. "Spot will keep you safe and help you not to be lonely."

Becky gently took the dog and cuddled him. Then she bent over and kissed Daniel. "Thank you, Daniel. I'm sure I'll be safe now." She paused before continuing, "I'll bring him home when we come to visit."

Daniel smiled and said, "Okay." Then he gave each of his big sisters a giant hug.

The girls drove off, with sixteen-year-old Darlene at the wheel. They planned to drive four hours to stay overnight with grandparents. Then they would drive the longer stretch the next day.

Four hours later my phone rang. "Mom, this is Becky. We had an accident, but we're okay."

"What happened?" I asked, concern filling my voice. "Darlene lost control of the car and flipped it over on the highway. The car rolled over. We're about one exit south of Grandmom's." Becky went on to explain a little more, including the fact that neither girl even had a scratch.

I breathed a sigh of relief. After I hung up, I said a silent prayer before phoning my in-laws, who immediately drove to the accident scene.

Daniel trotted in, half listening to the phone call, and asked, "What's the matter, Mom?"

"Your sisters had a car accident, but they're okay."

"I told you Spot would protect them."

"I'm afraid Becky will need another car, though."

My son responded with a serious look. "Do you think Spot's okay?" he asked.

I smiled at my young son and rumpled his hair. "I'm sure Spot's fine, too."

Daniel ran off to tell his other Beanie Babies about what happened to Spot.

My in-laws drove the girls to their destination. Days later, we arrived to help Becky settle in, buy a car, and bring Darlene home.

When we got home Darlene handed Spot to Daniel. He jumped up and down and hugged his little dog. "I'm glad you took Spot. He kept you safe."

Spot is now the family safety dog. He keeps an eye on all the travelers in our car.

*Sheri Gonzalez, age 12*

# Baby Blues

## BY SHANNON WOODWARD

**Z**ac hinted. He cajoled and pestered. He asked nicely. He gave daily updates. "Ben has two now, Mom. McKenna has a bunch." Finally, I relented. Zac got a Beanie Baby.

He already had a room full of toys. I didn't understand what all the fuss was about–or how he'd even notice one more stuffed animal.

Still, there was no denying his attachment to Peanut, the blue elephant. He talked to it. He gave it fourteen different names. It sat on the toilet seat while he took a bath. It sat on the table while he ate his cereal. Occasionally, I believe it had a nibble. At night, two heads rested on Zac's pillow. One was blue.

Nothing came close to overshadowing this attachment until our cat gave us a surprise of her own. One morning, we woke to find Frizzer purring contentedly in our closet with three just-born kittens. Those two pudgy, black fuzz balls and one teeny gray kitty were simply adorable.

We moved them to a basket and took turns admiring the newcomers. I wondered if the elephant would be forgotten in all the excitement, but Zac loyally brought him along on all visits.

One morning, we noticed a problem. The tiny gray kitten wasn't eating, meowing, or moving. We watched her all day, but she remained a lethargic little fluff ball. Sadly, the inevitable happened in the middle of the night. The next morning, we had a simple backyard service. Zac made a circle of rocks around the little grave and laid a bunch of forget-me-nots in the center.

"What is Frizzer going to think?" he asked. "What if she counts? She'll know one of her kittens is missing."

I didn't argue or tell him that cats can't count. I just hugged him.

That night, Zac came to the table without his ever-present elephant. I figured he was too upset about the kitten to remember the Beanie Baby.

He ate his dinner in silence. Near the end of the meal, he spoke for the first time.

"She can count now."

"What?"

"Frizzer. It's okay if she counts her babies now."

I went to the basket. There lay Frizzer curled around her three babies—two pudgy black kittens and one beloved blue elephant.

# Disappearing Blackie

BY LAURA DUVALL

In our house we have a collection of stuffed bears, and we enjoy setting them up in little groups. For example, one set of bears sits on a patchwork quilt enjoying a picnic. The bears have a basket of berries in front of them, a carrot cake, and a pot of tea, and they are dressed in their finest clothes. One little bear is a Beanie Baby named Blackie. He looks quite handsome in the purple velvet coat and cap we bought him.

But there have been some strange goings-on in our house at night, a mysterious occurrence we just couldn't figure out for the longest time. Every morning when I woke up I found Blackie in a different place. Sometimes he was in the upstairs hall, sometimes in the living room, and sometimes in the kitchen.

It never occurred to me that Sly, our gray and white blue-eyed cat, would have any interest in our bears. But one day as I picked Blackie up to return him to the picnic, I also picked up our cat and put him nose-to-nose with the Beanie Baby. To my surprise, Sly gave Blackie a kiss. And the next day, when my daughter Ashley came home from school, she found Blackie and Sly curled up together, taking a nap.

The secret was out! It was then that we knew the cat and bear were buddies. When we finally peeked one night, we saw our cat carrying the Beanie Baby in his mouth and taking him to another room. I giggle every time I think of Sly slipping off surreptitiously to retrieve Blackie in order to have a buddy beside him in the quiet hours of the night.

# As Time Goes By

## BY JUDI C. BRADDY

The streets of Old Folsom were vibrant with the colors and shapes of autumn. Corn stalks, pumpkins, and every variety of mum and marigold decorated the median on Main Street. They cast an earth-toned rainbow of orange, yellow, rust, and bronze against the century-old buildings.

One could almost wonder in the afternoon glow if daylight savings time had caused this place to fall back years rather than just an hour. The theme was duplicated in each specialty shop display window as I wandered casually down the wooden sidewalk savoring the combined atmosphere of California harvest and history.

When I reached a favorite shop whose name, "As Time Goes By," fit my mood of seasonal reflection, I turned in. Inside I watched a father, carrying a toddler, navigate two pre-school daughters deftly around the displays that would usually tempt youngsters. Heading straight to a corner brightly stocked with items for children, they were obviously on a mission. Absently I smiled and resumed my browsing.

A few minutes later they approached the register as I was paying for the two items I had been unable to resist.

"Excuse me," the young father addressed the proprietor. "Do you have Peking, the panda bear?" I glanced at the two preschoolers at his side who waited for the answer with large expectant eyes.

"I'm sorry," she answered, "if there are none on the shelf we must have sold the last one." Then she added, half to him, half to me, "Boy, those went fast!"

It was just then that I noticed two small pandas on a display wall behind the counter and asked if those could be the ones they were looking for.

A bright look crossed the faces, then disappointment. "No," came a small lisping voice, "the oneths we want are Beanie Babies—thoseth are not the thame."

Immediately I understood, and my mind replayed a similar scene twenty years ago, only the roles were reversed. This time as a young mother I walked down the aisle of a large toy store, carrying my three-year old son with two other small boys in tow.

It was the fourth store we'd been to and it, too, was completely sold out of Jawas—the latest, just-released action figure from the *Star Wars* movie. Hundreds of other action figures hung on display, but they weren't the "thame."

What we choose to collect most certainly tells something about each generation's times and trends. For me, and every other kid growing up in the fifties, it was cowboys, Indians, and horses. I can remember my mother and I going from store to store to find a porcelain horse that was different from the rest of my collection.

I have come to understand over the years that part of the joy of collecting—be it Beanie Babies, action figures, or horses—often has as much to do with the finding as it does with the having. Though it may be that acquiring every new collectible is the most important quest at the time, the childhood memories that are ultimately connected to those things will only come into proper perspective as experience presses us into adulthood.

Each porcelain horse riding on the white clouds of a Kansas summer afternoon allowed a child to believe that someday she'd have a horse of her very own. Each molded and painted action figure reminded a boy of an afternoon *Star Wars* matinee with his dad. And perhaps a floppy, furry friend will eventually evoke a memory of the golden autumn day in Old Folsom when a father and his daughters went to just one more store looking for that special panda to add to the collection of other Beanies.

As I turned to leave the shop I heard the father say they would have to look someplace else. I looked at those little ones and thought of my own grandchildren. There had to be a shop nearby where I, too, could find those pandas for my grandchildren's collection of Beanie Babies and memories.

# Princess Changes the World

BY LAURA WHITE

♥ ♥ ♥

**C**an a Beanie Baby named Princess really change the world? Perhaps she can.

Princess is one of the hardest Beanies to find, making her highly sought after by Beanie Baby collectors. Some say that she commemorates Princess Diana's life, which makes her even more valuable.

World Relief decided to auction this special bear to raise money to help poor children under the age of five. The money was to be distributed in countries with unusually high childhood death rates. But the problem was—where would they find the illusive Princess?

The World Relief president, Dr. Clive Calver, was planning a trip to Great Britain last Easter. He was to address more than 60,000 people at Spring Harvest, the largest gathering of European evangelical Christians. The task of finding the purple bear fell on him, but it was no easy task. Calver and his wife, Ruth, spent an afternoon combing London's shopping district for the bear. At the seventh shop, the search was over.

"I didn't expect Beanie Babies to be part of this job. But if the auction of Princess can help care for the poor and the sick, then I will enthusiastically participate!" Calver declared.

He hand-carried Princess from London to Wheaton, Illinois, where the auction took place. She was auctioned off for $150, the approximate cost of helping three children survive to age five in third-world countries such as Cambodia, Mozambique, and Nicaragua.

Development experts agree that in poor countries the first five years of a child's life are most critical. Once children survive to age five, their risk of early death drops significantly. That is why many relief organizations concentrate on helping children at an early age.

Appropriately, a proud kindergarten graduate is the new owner of this special Princess.

The rewards are tantalizing. Ken and Patti Fisher of Richwood, Kentucky found the "Holy Grail" of Beanie Babies—-a royal blue, mint condition Peanuts the elephant. They bought it for $2,500. Within four months, the estimated value soared to $7,500.

# My Buddy

BY SARA MCDONNALL

♥ ♥ ♥

Flying back home to Colorado from Atlanta, Georgia, I had a three-hour wait at the airport. Since my traveling companions had all caught earlier flights, and I was alone, I meandered through the echoing concourse, browsing through the various shops. Suddenly, a feeling of isolation crept over me.

Celebration and excitement had marked the last three days. An international company brought high school students from across the nation together for an award trip in Atlanta. Now as I headed home, the letdown descended upon me.

*If I only had a friend here with me, I would not be so lonely*, I reasoned to myself.

Just then my backpack brushed against a display. I felt something fall to the floor, and as I turned to pick it up, my eyes caught the familiar Beanie Baby tag. My heart melted as my fingers closed around the adorable little puppy, wearing his heart on a string around his neck. On his tag, cheerful letters spelled out his name, Fetch.

From that moment on, Fetch and I were traveling companions. He kept me company on the long flight home and throughout the remainder of the summer. I had a friend with me wherever I went.

When I started my freshman year of college in the fall, Fetch made the long trek with me across the country once again. Even now, he sits on my desk, cheering me up during those hard times when it seems I am once again wandering alone through the halls of life. Only now I am not alone; I have my Fetch with me.

# Kayla's Promise

## BY JAN WILLIAMS

❤ ❤ ❤

"Tomorrow is Saturday. When you wake up in the morning, you need to be quiet. It's grandma's day to sleep in. Okay?" I said to my two-year-old granddaughter, Kayla Rose.

"Yes, Grandma," she dutifully replied, though I could see by the mischievous look in her eyes she had no intention of keeping her promise.

The word precocious was coined for Kayla. At her tender age, her vocabulary is mind boggling. She is also creative. She has turned cardboard boxes into homes for all her Beanie Baby friends. During the day she tends them regularly, and before she says her prayers, she tucks each one into bed for the night.

I stood beside her bed, along with her mother and father that evening, listening to her prayers.

"Now I lay me down to sleep," her mother started, and Kayla chimed in quickly, along with her.

She said, "Amen," as the last word of that well-known prayer was spoken. Then Kayla began the lengthy process of asking God to bless her extensive human family. Soon thereafter, she asked God to bless all of her Beanie Babies, each by name. Then she moved on to all her other stuffed animals. Twenty minutes later the last of the squeezable furry friends had been blessed. Only then did my cherub-faced granddaughter slip into bed.

"Did I bless everything when I was that young?" my daughter asked, reaching back to turn out the light.

"Probably not. You didn't have such a collection of friends," I added with a smile.

Before turning out the hall lights, I reminded my daughter it was my Saturday to sleep in, just in case it had slipped her mind. She smiled that smile—the one she wore when I was asking for something absurd.

"Did you tell Kayla?" she asked.

I nodded and shut my bedroom door.

The following morning I awoke to a house so quiet it frightened me. It was eight o'clock and time for my dog to poke her wet nose in my face. I looked beside the bed. She wasn't in the room. She must have gone out with my husband earlier.

Then I glanced at the pillow my husband had vacated earlier. There lay my granddaughter, tucked beneath the covers, Beanies spread all around her. Her eyes were wide open. When our eyes met, an impish smile spread across her face. Kayla had kept her promise. She and her Beanies had patiently waited for grandma to wake up.

# Beanie Babies to the Rescue

## BY IRENE TAYLOR

❤ ❤ ❤

"**O**h no! Not again!"
"This is no fun!"
"Do we have to?"

It was that time of the school year again—standardized testing week! Those cries from my fourth grade students met me one sunny April morning, and I was inclined to agree with them.

Our school, as do many others, puts a great deal of emphasis on these test scores, so we encourage the children to do well. For many years, testing week has become a stressful one for the students and teachers. But last year was different. It was Beanie Babies to the rescue!

As a way to deal with this stressful week, my fourth graders came up with the idea of creating a Beanie Baby "good luck cheering section." Each morning the students brought in their favorite Beanies. Some brought one, some brought a few, and some even brought extras to share with the few students who did not have Beanie Babies of their own. I was temporarily given my own Beanie Baby each day to help me through the testing week, too.

Each morning we created a huge gallery on the bookshelf where the Beanie Babies and the students had a good view of each other. As the testing sessions progressed, students could look to the Beanie Gallery and find the quiet support of their favorite Beanie Babies. Just having those smiling faces to look at during anxious moments made everyone feel better.

Did our Beanie Baby gallery make a difference in the test scores? Well, the students worked hard, did a great job, and achieved terrific scores. Who is to say how much difference those Beanie Babies made, but feeling relaxed, happy, and in the company of someone you love surely didn't hurt!

McDonald's Teenie Beanie Baby promotion in April 1997 was planned for four weeks, but the supply of Teenie Beanies sold out in two weeks. The next promotion occurred a year later, on May 22, 1998. Interestingly, McDonald's and Ty, Inc. are both located in Oak Brook, Illinois.

# Be Careful What You Say

BY MELISSA MARCHIONNA (AGE 12)

♥ ♥ ♥

It all started when Erin, the St. Patty's day bear, was really, really hard to find. My mom and I walked into a local store selling Beanie Babies and discovered that they were holding a raffle for Erin. If your name was drawn, you had the opportunity to purchase Erin for the low price of fifteen dollars.

My mom and I, of course, both put our names in. On our way out of the store, my mom saw some people she knew, and she asked them if they would enter their names so I would have a better chance of winning.

The next day at church, my mother asked Father Paul, our Irish priest, if he would also enter his name in the raffle. One of the other priests overheard us and said, "I think there are more important things to be seeking, like the kingdom of God perhaps."

My mom turned to him and said, "Father, you're not twelve!"

Anyway, Father Paul did enter his name in the raffle just for me.

A couple of days later Mom and I returned to the Beanie Baby store to enter my dad's name.

The man at the counter said, "Let me tell you about your competition. You've got a woman whose birthday is the same day as the drawing. And you have an Irish Catholic priest!"

My mom and I started to laugh, and then Mom explained, "The priest is with us."

Unfortunately, my name was never picked for the raffle, but a couple of weeks later Father Paul approached us after Mass one Sunday and mentioned that he would soon be going to Europe. What a perfect chance to pick up

*Emily Hu*

the Britannia bear! My mom described the bear in full detail and told Father Paul where to purchase it.

After all her careful instructions Father Paul turned to Mom and said, "Dearie, I'll get that bear even if I have to steal it!"

Just then, a deacon walked into the room and said "Father, do you know that your mike is on?"

# Aunt Kay's Priceless Gift

## BY KIM B. BISHOP

❤ ❤ ❤

**M**any parents experience the agony of watching and waiting while a little child suffers through an illness. It is a time unlike any other; suddenly life's priorities are clearly defined. Sickness hushes the laughter and chatter that were the music of the playroom, while loyal little toys wait patiently for the return of their playmate.

Melissa, now just four, lay still on the couch. Her gaze was fixed on nothing, her body burning with fever. In too much pain to cry, she managed a tiny whimper. As parents, we were beside ourselves with concern. We had tried to soothe the hurt, cool the fever—but to no avail.

Pleading prayers from a mother's heart were silently offered up. I immediately thought of Aunt Kay and realized that she was the answer to my prayers. Kay is the essence of compassion and care. Kindness is simply her lifestyle. It is little wonder she became a medical doctor.

The doorbell rang before we hardly hung up the phone. There stood Kay in the doorway with a smile, an otoscope, and a Beanie Baby.

After examining Melissa, writing a prescription, and reassuring worried parents, Kay tucked Pounce, a little brown and tan stuffed kitten, under our baby girl's limp arm— medicine for the heart.

Melissa's eyes suddenly lit up with a Christmas-like glow, and she cuddled the kitty closer to her. The fever and aches seemed to drain right out of her. Then she simply drifted off into a healing sleep, the precious toy with the red heart tag nestled to her cheek.

*Sheri Gonzalez, age 12*

What is the value of this child's small toy? I have heard that serious collectors price the rarest of these Beanie Babies in the thousands of dollars, particularly if they are considered in "mint condition." But on that day of fevers and fears, of prayers being answered through an angel aunt, and the never-to-be-forgotten image of a sleeping child clinging to a little animal, I would say its value is . . . priceless.

# Things to Do:
# A Magic Flying Carpet

BY KAREN H. WHITING

💙 💙 💙

Have you wondered what you can do to join your children in playing with Beanie Babies? Well here is an idea that worked magically for me. Plus, it entertained my eight-year-old son for an entire morning.

"Daniel, I made you a surprise," I said one morning.

"What is it, Mom?" he asked, racing into the room.

"It's a flying carpet for your Beanie Babies," I replied.

"Wow! How does it work."

"Go get Bongo, and I'll show you."

Daniel ran upstairs to find his little brown monkey. Seconds later he bounded down the stairs, clutching his Beanie Baby.

Daniel placed Bongo in the center of the large scarf carpet. He tightly held the two cardboard control rods and swung Bongo on the flying carpet.

"Bongo won't fall off and get hurt, will he?" Daniel asked. I smiled at my young son's thoughtfulness. "No, I think he'll like the ride. He can pretend he's traveling to far away places.

💙 138 💙

"He'll get lonely riding by himself. He needs a friend." Daniel gently landed Bongo on the floor and ran off again. Quickly he returned with Bernie, his St. Bernard.

All morning, Daniel took his Beanie Babies on trips around the world and into outer space. Bongo and Bernie peeked out to see the view around them, as they whirled past tables and chairs, lamps, and sofas.

Every so often, the Beanie Babies experienced turbulence in the ride as Daniel bounced the flying carpet up and down in the air. Still, the two sat quietly, content to travel anywhere their pilot flew them.

Daniel announced, "Coming in for a landing," as he slowed the carpet down and gently landed it on the floor. He took out his passengers, rolled up the carpet, and announced, "Time for lunch, Bongo and Bernie."

❤ ❤ ❤

# Make a Beanie Baby Flying Carpet

BY KAREN H. WHITING

## MATERIALS:

Large silk scarf or fabric square
String
2 pieces of mat board, or heavy cardboard, 1.5" x 12"
   (control rods)
4 large beads with holes

### DIRECTIONS:

❤ Punch a hole one-inch from each end of the cardboard piece. Cut two pieces of string, 36" long.

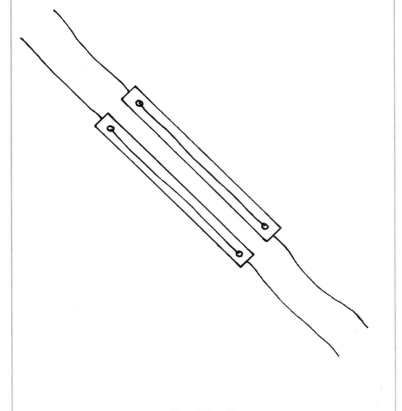

❤ Push each corner of the scarf through a hole in a bead.

❤ Knot the scarf.

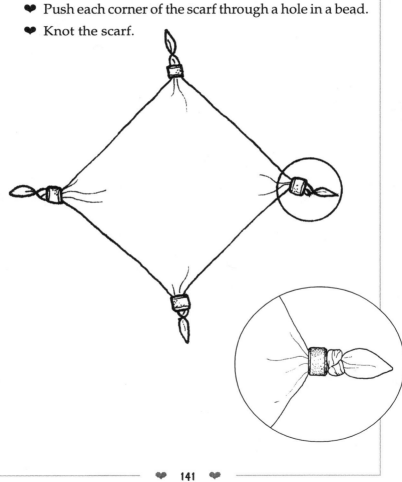

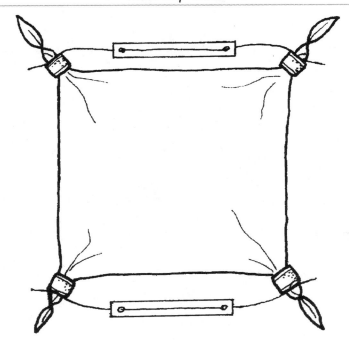

❤ Tie one end of the string to a corner of the scarf, below the bead.

❤ Run the string in one hole and out the other hole of a control rod.

❤ Tie the end to the adjacent corner of the scarf.

❤ Repeat attaching string and control rod to the other two corners.

❤ Flying: Hold the two control rods apart to allow the carpet to open. Place Beanie Babies in the center. Swing arms to move the carpet through the air.

# Beanie Babies Land Dad a Job

## BY MARIA DUSENBERY

❤ ❤ ❤

**O**ur story begins on Sanibel Island in Florida. While we were vacationing there we met Kristina Walker, an eight-year-old girl who was also on vacation with her family. Kristina had recently received Princess from her parents as a special gift. She cherished this Beanie Baby—slept with it, loved it, and wore it out a bit.

When our vacation was over we returned home to Michigan. My kids stayed in touch with Kristina. They told her that they couldn't buy their own Princess because their dad had just lost his job. When Kristina sold Girl Scout cookies for her troop we ordered some. When the box arrived in the mail my kids tore into it to sample the goodies. But they found more than just cookies. They also found a well-loved Princess bear.

Kristina felt sad that my two kids couldn't afford a Princess of their own, so she sent them hers. We immediately called her to thank her for her generosity, though we didn't feel right taking her precious Beanie Baby.

"It's okay," she said, "because my dad just donated

money to a woman's shelter, and they're giving us a new Princess to thank us."

The story doesn't end there, however. A couple of months later Kristina's dad contacted my husband and provided him with an opportunity to start a business. Beanie Babies gave joy to our three children, taught our family a wonderful lesson about generosity, and even provided a job for my husband. Princess, and all the other Beanies we have collected, holds a special place in our hearts.

*Samantha King, age 12*

# Freckles to the Rescue

## BY MIDGE DESART

❤ ❤ ❤

It was a mother's worst fear come true. I answered the phone to learn that my thirty-two-year-old son, Scott, had been injured at work. He had fallen from the top of a twenty-foot ladder. The good news was he landed on his feet. The bad news was he had broken both legs in the fall.

What followed were nine hours of surgery—and nine hours of praying and waiting. I remained with Scott the first night after surgery because his wife needed to stay at home with their two small children.

During the long vigil, I paced the hospital hallways. On one of these walks I stumbled upon the gift shop. A sign in the window announced that Beanie Babies would arrive the following day. I had recently purchased my first Beanie Baby and was just learning how hard it was to find them.

The next morning I was first in line when the gift shop opened. I bought a handful of adorable Beanie Babies and returned to my son's room.

By this time Scott was conscious and experiencing a great deal of pain. The lights bothered him. He tried to find something to cover his eyes to achieve total darkness. Wash cloths kept falling off, and towels were too bulky. That's when I showed him the Beanie Babies I had just purchased. He whispered through his pain, "They're cute. Can I hold one?"

I handed him Freckles the leopard. Beanie Babies are not only soft to the touch, but they mold to the palm of the hand or shoulder—wherever they're placed. After turning him around in his hand, Scott slowly draped Freckles over his eyes. It was exactly what he needed. Freckles shielded him from the intrusive light and gave him a chance to rest more comfortably.

When my grandchildren were finally able to visit their daddy, they were impressed that Grandma had given him a toy of his own to help him get better. For Easter that year I gave the children their own Beanie Babies. Scott continues to keep little Freckles nearby as a reminder of how a little furry critter helped ease his pain.

---

"Old Face" Teddies vs. "New Face" Teddies: The original Teddies had a long, snout-like muzzle with eyes facing slightly away from the front of the face. The new Teddies were redesigned to have round faces, with eyes closer together facing forward; they also enjoyed the addition of a colorful neck ribbon.

# Christmas Surprise

## BY HEATHER MERLUCCI

**A** local flower shop in my hometown was holding a raffle for a Christmas tree decorated in Beanie Babies. It was December 1997, and at that time the Christmas Teddy was hard to find.

The flower shop was not expecting to receive any of the new Beanies in time for the Christmas tree raffle. However, I had two 1997 Christmas Teddies in my collection, and when I stopped in at the florist shop I noticed that the Christmas tree had no Beanie Baby on top.

I called the shop that weekend and offered to donate my Christmas Teddy for the top of their tree. The owner was quite grateful. She said she had never seen such a heart-warming gesture. I was hoping a child would win the raffle so he or she could not only get a new tree but also the 1997 Christmas Teddy.

I walked over to the shop and hand delivered the Beanie Baby. Just as I was about to leave, I noticed the raffle box and decided to enter my name. Well, wouldn't you know that my name was the one that was chosen. I won the Christmas tree! So I called a local rescue shelter and asked if I could donate a Christmas tree to add some Yuletide spirit to their center.

The shelter director was thrilled. "This will warm everybody's heart," she said. "It's just what's needed when the weather is so awfully cold."

"I'd like to insist on one thing, however," I said. "Please be sure the children get the Beanie Babies. It would be wonderful to think that all the children could snuggle up with cuddly critters all their own when Christmas morning rolls around."

*Myles Ellison, age 10*

She nodded. "I know it will put a sparkle in their eyes," the shelter director said with a smile.

As I walked out of the shelter I couldn't help smiling. One little donated Beanie Baby had blossomed into a wonderful gift for a group of people who could surely use some Christmas cheer.

# Maternal Instinct

BY MELISSA HURLEY (AGE 13)

♥ ♥ ♥

I once had a cat named Skippity Do Da, Skippity A who slept in my room at night. His carpeted kitty house sat in one corner of my bedroom. One night when I went to sleep I took two Beanie Baby kittens to bed with me. Skippity Do Da Skippity A was in his usual place curled up asleep when I turned the light out.

The next morning when I woke up my Beanie kittens were right beside Skippity Do Da Skippity A in his house. It looked just like kittens snuggling up to a mother cat. I couldn't imagine how they got there. At first I thought my mom and dad or brother and sister had played a joke on me, but when I reached in to take the Beanie kittens away, Skippity Do Da Skippity A bit me. I immediately dropped the Beanie kitten.

Skippity picked up the kitten by the scruff of its neck and carried it to the other side of the room. Then he came back, picked up the other kitten, and carried it to the new location. After that he proceeded to clean them just like a mother cat cleans her kittens. I could see that my Beanie Baby kittens didn't need me any more. They had finally found a mom—or was it a dad?

# Grandapanda

BY RAMONA JEAN WOLFE

💜 💜 💜

I was a successful interior designer with a busy career until ten years ago when a nineteen-year-old boy hit my car head on. For the next year I was confined to bed with a condition known as traumatic brain injury (TBI).

My busy and fulfilling life had suddenly come to a halt. It was difficult to concentrate, and I couldn't find anything that sparked my interest.

Then one day a friend brought a large box of Beanie Babies to my house. I looked at the huge mound of little animals and wondered if she had lost her mind.

We talked a while. She said she bought five hundred dollars worth and that I could buy some from her. I reached into the box and pulled out a cute little lamb with a smiling pink face. Her name was Fleece, and she tugged at my heartstrings. "I think I'd like to have this lamb," I said rather matter-of-factly.

My friend smiled and beckoned me to reach into the pile one more time.

Next I pulled out a cute little cocker spaniel named Spunky. "We used to have a dog. She looked kind of like this. I'll take this one, too." My voice was starting to sound more enthusiastic.

Just then I noticed a brown and white squirrel with a big bushy tail. I thought back to happy times of feeding the squirrels in the park. I immediately fell in love with Nuts, too, and my Beanie hunt began.

It wasn't long before my grandchildren, my daughter, and my mother all got involved. One time I took my mother with me to a store to try to purchase Princess. We were the tenth and eleventh people in line. My mother started to laugh.

I looked at her quizzically and asked, "What are you laughing about?"

She replied, "I have stood in long lines twice in my life: once during the war for beans to eat and now for beans to look at."

I laughed, but I'll have to admit I'm hooked. I love the hunt for hard to locate Beanies, but the find is the ultimate high. I take anyone who will go with me to search for the illusive ones. I will drive two hours one way if I hear of a place that might have Beanie Babies I'm looking for.

At this time I have 148 Beanie Babies. I have made one of my bedrooms into a Beanie room. I display my Beanies in different locations around the room. They really provide a cheerful atmosphere. I allow the grandchildren to play with most of them. And when I'm not feeling well, I sit and relax in this room. Just being around my Beanies makes me feel so much better.

# Beanie Sisters

## BY SHANNON CHRISTENSEN

❤ ❤ ❤

I love my little sister, but we have always struggled with finding common interests since I am sixteen years older. I am twenty-eight, and Ann-Marie is twelve.

That problem was happily resolved, however, last May when I discovered Beanie Babies. Many of my friends were collecting Beanies, and it was all they could talk about. I felt so left out. At the time I wondered if that was how my sister had felt when my friends and I talked about subjects in front of her that didn't hold her interest.

I decided to learn about Beanies so I went shopping and purchased my first Beanie Babies. I came home with Dotty, Smoochy, and Mystic. I thought they were cute, but was later informed that I should have purchased the "retired" Beanies. I didn't even know what a retired one was. I had much to learn.

My sister offered to help me because she had developed an interest in Beanies, too. Ann-Marie and I visited the Internet and learned how to collect them.

Today we spend our Saturdays hunting for Beanies. Once we acquired most of the May retirees, our next target was the bears. By accident I stumbled across Peace, Valentino, and Curly for five dollars each. Then a few weeks later I found Princess and Erin, too. Now I have over fifty-eight Beanies. My husband thinks I am crazy, but my sister and I are hooked. There is no turning back!

I've been lucky in finding older Beanies. I won Goldie in a contest, got Cubbie from a friend, and bought Nip at a sale on the beach. I may never be able to afford all of the older Beanies, but it is fun to try and find them at a reasonable price!

Collecting Beanies has brought my little sister and I closer together. We love to talk Beanies, read Beanie magazines, and shop together. Beanies have strengthened the bond between us, and I treasure the closeness we share today.

Princess Bear: Ty, Inc. received official approval to design a bear to honor the memory of Princess Diana. The purple "Princess" bear, bearing an embroidered white rose on the right side of her chest, was released on December 1, 1997. All proceeds are donated to the Princess of Wales Memorial Fund.

# Man's Best Friend

BY GLENDA LANGFORD

**M**y foray into the world of Beanie Babies began in August 1998, but it would never have happened if it weren't for the adorable Beanie poodle named Gigi. Most people who are familiar with Beanie Babies, and Gigi in particular, like her because she is a cute little puppy. But I love Gigi because of the wonderful memories I have of another black poodle named Chigger. Chigger and I grew up together and, since I was an only child, Chigger was my brother and sister and beloved pet all rolled into one.

When I was thirteen years old my mother was diagnosed with cancer. For five and a half years all of us struggled with her illness before she died. During that time Chigger became her trusted companion. When she needed something to eat or drink, Chigger would come and bark at me. When the pain became so great she couldn't sleep, Chigger would gently climb up beside her on her hospital bed. His presence and warmth would relax her, and this allowed her to finally fall asleep. Sometimes, after she was sleeping soundly, Chigger would come into my room and lie down with a forlorn look on his face as if he knew what was unfolding.

My father had always said he never wanted a housedog, but when he saw how Chigger doted on my mother, he vowed he would take good care of Chigger for the rest of his days. Even though he was seventeen years old and could not walk or see very well, Chigger was there to watch me walk down the aisle on my wedding day.

One month later, on Christmas, Chigger passed away. Now that I was married and on my own he realized his job was over. His long years as a devoted servant to both my mother and me was completed. I'll never forget that sweet dog. And when I spotted Gigi on the shelf amongst many other colorful critters, she brought back all the wonderful memories of my faithful pal Chigger. I knew I had to have that little beanbag dog as a gentle reminder of Chigger's loving presence in our lives.

Smoochy is my favorite. I like his green color and his cool eyes.

Submitted by Tanner Leonhardt (age 6)

# Beanies Here, Beanies There, Beanies Everywhere

BY TRUDY PARKS

♥ ♥ ♥

I am a fifty-year-old grandmother who has recently started collecting Beanie Babies. What's really neat about this hobby is that my two granddaughters, Ashley and Stephanie, ages eleven and twelve, are helping me to find my "treasures." Whenever we go places together, we're on the lookout for new members of our Beanie family.

The girls are as enthusiastic about my collection as I am. We often go to doll shows. We have discovered that there are more and more Beanies offered at these shows. When we arrive I tell the girls which Beanie Babies I am looking for, and off they go looking for the best bargains they can find. They are more excited than I am when it comes to the Beanie hunt!

Not only do I have fun spending time with my granddaughters, but I am teaching them valuable lessons. They are learning to get the best bargains for their money. They've learned not to buy the first thing they see because they may find the same Beanie later in the day. I love the way this pastime brings us together—all working for that "ultimate find."

My mobile home is getting so filled with all my collectibles that I'll have to go sleep out in the shed one of these days. I have Beanies here, Beanies there, and Beanies everywhere! They are so cute that I can't resist them. The neighborhood kids come to see them and to check if I have bought any new ones. Beanie Babies are definitely keeping me young.

# Beanies in Therapy

## BY DIANE BISHOP

❤ ❤ ❤

I am one of those moms who swore she would never let her children get caught up in the Beanie Baby craze, but now that we have over a hundred of them, I'd better explain.

Almost two years ago, our six-year-old son, Scott, was undergoing speech therapy. He made great progress as long as he was doing repetitive drills with Karen, his therapist. But when it came time for him to practice these sounds in conversation, Karen found it difficult to entice our shy son to talk.

But then we discovered a solution—Beanie Babies! One time I let Scott take one of his Beanie Babies to a speech therapy session. When I picked him up, Karen couldn't conceal her excitement. She was ecstatic over how much he had talked that day—all about his Beanie Babies. He loved their poems and their names and that they all had their own birthdays. From then on, I was happy to get Scott more Beanies; he would take two or three of them with him to each session. Karen would make up games with the

*Patrick Stevens, age 10*

Beanies and chat about the ones he had and the ones he wanted.

Even after he was released from speech therapy, Scott asked to visit Karen to show her any new Beanies he might have acquired. I was thrilled and never would have imagined that Beanies could be used as such a valuable therapeutic tool.

# The Wrinkle-Faced Pug

BY ROSALIE CAMPBELL

❤ ❤ ❤

Few things excite a woman as much as the adventure of checking out a new mall in a new city, or for that matter, any mall in any city.

While on vacation in North Carolina recently, I discovered that a mall was within walking distance from our hotel. I lured my reluctant husband to join me in one of my favorite pastimes—shopping.

As we entered the multi-leveled retail complex, I spotted a Beanie Babies sign on a stand in the middle of the wide promenade. "Wow!" I exclaimed, "Look at the variety. That stand's loaded."

Stan sighed and looked for the nearest bench, as I rushed over to inspect the colorful collection of Beanies.

The plush animals were squeezed together on several shelves. One pair of shiny black eyes drew my attention. I picked up a curly-tailed, fawn-colored creature. His pushed-in, wrinkled black face seemed to grin at me. The name on the hangtag said Pugsly.

"That pug looks just like Brandon's dog," I said to myself. Even though my son was thirty-six, I knew he would love Pugsly as much as I did since it looked exactly like Skipper. I had to buy him!

I hurried over to show Stan my new purchase. His eyes lit up when he saw Pugsly. "It looks just like Brandon's dog," he commented.

Skipper came into Brandon's life at a time when my son desperately needed a friend. His health was deteriorating. His weight and energy kept dwindling. Brandon's emotional level decreased daily as he fought the battle with AIDS. Ultimately he had to give up his job and his apartment. At thirty-two, Brandon was forced to return home to live with his parents. He needed something or someone to boost his spirits.

When mulling over his situation, Brandon concluded that a dog might be the answer to his loneliness. He researched the characteristics of many breeds. When he discovered that pugs show lots of affection, are playful, are small, and make good house pets, the decision was made. He would buy a pug.

Skipper fit the bill. He displayed lots of personality along with a curious grin and a feisty stance. He brought sunshine into a dark time of my son's life. Skipper offered Brandon the gift of friendship. Perhaps this little pug Beanie would be a reminder of Skipper's faithfulness and love.

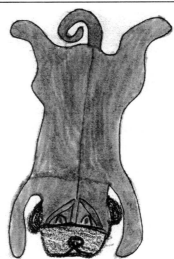

This is my favorite beanie baby, pugsley. I Love pugsley, because I own a pugdog and her name is Phoebe. I Love thier curly tails. Blake Leonhart Age 9

*Blake Leonhart, age 9*

# Sharing the Fun

BY CHRIS JUDGE (AGE 11)

❤ ❤ ❤

**M**om and my sisters love Beanie Babies just like I do. One day Mom was at a Beanie show. At one booth a man was selling Beanies without their hangtags for two dollars each! My three-year-old sister who loves Beanies had ripped the tags off every Beanie she owns. She had even gotten hold of some of Mom's retireds, so Mom wanted to buy her more of her own. Of course my sister wanted every Beanie the man was selling, so Mom ended up buying her thirteen of them.

The next day Mom answered an ad in the *Ty Guestbook* from a man who was looking for inexpensive Beanies for his five-year-old daughter to play with. Mom found out that the little girl had been a big sister for only a week, and her dad wanted a special gift for her.

Mom remembered how the man at the Beanie show had sold her two dollar Beanies, and she found it in her heart to send the Beanies to the little girl. She fixed up a special package and even included a Beanie belt for the little girl to carry her treasured friends on.

The father said, "My daughter was thrilled with the package. How much do I owe you?"

Mom replied, "There's no charge, but keep me in mind when you are Beanie hunting. My son is raising two guide dogs for the blind. His first faithful companion, Fran, is due to go back for formal training in a couple of weeks. He will never see her again. I know that

*Shelby Osborn, age 5*

"turn-in" will be difficult. I want to buy Princess as a special gift for him."

Mom wanted to give me something to remind me of Fran and how I had trained her. She asked the man if he came across Princess to please purchase her for me. Later Mom discovered that the man already owned Princess! He sent me a bear in mint condition for free because of my duty for training my guide dog.

He said, "If Chris at eleven can give that much to his community, I can give up Princess."

Now is that a special person, or what?

# A Little Luck

## BY ADRIENNE GELFIUS

❤ ❤ ❤

"**H**ere," I said, as I handed my sister Kelly the ladybug named Lucky. "I bought this for you—for good luck with your medical tests tomorrow." She took the small, red beanbag animal from my outstretched hand and read the tag.

"Aw, her name is Lucky," she said with a sigh.

"Not that you need luck. Everything will be fine, I'm sure." I smiled and touched her shoulder. I felt badly for her when I saw her stare down at the small memento and blink back tears. Tomorrow she would undergo extensive medical tests, and she was understandably concerned.

"Thank you," she said as she smiled up at me.

Mom had called me the day before to tell me the bad news. During a chest x-ray doctors had discovered three small spots on Kelly's lungs. She would need to undergo a needle biopsy to see what they were, and it didn't look good.

"I'll take Lucky with me to the hospital tomorrow," she said. All that evening Kelly kept the ladybug beside her.

The next few days were difficult as we waited for the

results. I jumped when the phone rang.

"I'm fine. The doctors think it's the result of an infection, but definitely not cancer." Kelly's voice was noticeably upbeat over the phone.

"I'm so relieved," I said.

Having been diagnosed with diabetes twenty-eight years ago, Kelly has been through innumerable medical treatments. As the years pass, her medical problems have seemed to grow more frequent and serious. Receiving Lucky, however, seemed to lift her spirits and give her renewed hope.

*Kimberly Reinhardt, age 12*

Though Kelly had never heard of Beanie Babies before receiving Lucky, she now enjoys collecting them as much as I do. In fact, she now fills *me* in on the latest Beanie information and has a collection that rivals my own. And to think it all started with her need for a little luck.

# Empty Nesters

## BY KATHY SMITH

**W**hen my youngest child went away to college my biggest fear was realized. My husband and I had been so busy raising a family we forgot to spend time with each other. We now had little in common. We found the times we communicated most were when we were talking about our children.

It was during this transitional stage that I began buying a few Beanie Babies here and there. I was by no means a serious collector. I did it primarily for my son who was in college. He enjoyed collecting some of the zanier looking creatures.

One day we received a call from our son. He asked his dad if he would go on a quest for a special Beanie Baby that he wanted to give a friend. Since my husband knows less than I do about Beanie Babies, he asked me to come along and join him in the search.

Well, we never did find the Beanie my son had requested, but we did find some common ground. We've spent many hours searching for the hard-to-find retired critters and, in the process, rekindled our interest in one another. Now we

*Nick Anthony, age 11*

not only hunt for Beanie Babies together, we also spend a great deal of time enjoying one another's company. We have learned to share interests other than our children. In the process, we have bought many a captivating Beanie Baby. Our home has become a happy "Beanie Haven."

# Share Time

## BY DONNA GETZINGER

❤ ❤ ❤

**M**y students can't wait for Mondays. It's share time. They talk about it all week long. Which toy should they bring to school to share with the class?

Deciding what to bring, however, was not a problem for one boy, Sam, who always brought the same thing—a cute grey, beanbag shark. The first time Sam shared the shark it was brand new. His friends liked it.

Colin, the Beanie Baby expert in our class, told us that the shark's name was Crunch. "All the names are on the tags," Colin pointed out.

Sam, however, being dyslexic, hadn't been able to read the tag. "I call him Jaws," Sam said, "like the movie."

"But that's not his name," Colin insisted. The other children agreed with Colin. Giving the shark another name was apparently against the rules. But Sam continued to call him Jaws.

The following Monday Sam brought Jaws in for share time again. This really bothered the class.

"You shared that last week," Colin and the others complained. They refused to listen to Sam's latest shark adventures. Instead, they focused on Colin's newest Lego creation.

A week later, Jaws appeared again, but Colin upstaged the lone shark with a backpack full of Beanie Babies. He had crammed at least fifteen stuffed animals in his sack, including a correctly named shark.

"I have more at home," Colin said. "I'm trying to get every one."

The dismissal bell rang before Colin could share his entire collection. As a result, Sam and several other children didn't get a chance to talk about their precious toys. I promised them that they could share the next day. Sam beamed. He'd get to bring Jaws to school two days in a row!

From October straight through the holidays, and even after winter break, Sam still shared his cuddly shark while the other children brought in new toys.By January some of the shark's color had been hugged away and the heart-shaped tag ripped off. Sam explained that the tag bothered him at night when he slept with the shark.

"It's not worth anything without the tag," Colin explained. "When it's retired, you won't get anything for it."

"I don't want to get anything for it," Sam said. "I want to keep it."

Colin and the other children rolled their eyes. "You don't get it at all," Colin said.

Sam may have been unaware of the potential monetary value of the stuffed animal, but of all the students I've ever had, Sam understood most clearly the value of a cherished object. He knew that some things can't be judged in dollars and cents. Watching Sam, I have no doubt that he will some day be the kind of friend we all would want. Sam did get it, after all!

Crunch the Shark

Jessica Freitas

*Jessica Freitas, age 7*

# A Special Gift for Kody

## BY KIM ROTHENBECK

❤ ❤ ❤

**M**y son Kody has spina bifida. When he was only thirteen, he was scheduled to have his third scoliosis surgery in three years to help straighten his back. To take his mind off his medical concerns, I introduced him to Beanie Babies, and he became an avid collector.

I've made friends with some of the storeowners on my Beanie hunts. I always talk about my son and how he likes to collect Beanies.

One of the storeowners wanted to meet my son so I promised I would bring Kody in as soon as possible. A few weeks later, we were in the neighborhood so I brought Kody in to meet my friend. We talked about his upcoming surgery.

My friend reached up and grabbed a frog Beanie off the shelf and threw it to Kody saying, "Here. This is for good luck with your surgery."

My son hugged Smoochy and thanked the storeowner. His thoughtfulness meant so much to me, too.

On the way home Kody read Smoochy's tag and checked

This is Smoochy.

I like his green color and his cool eyes. Tanner Leonhardt Age 6

*Tanner Leonhardt, age 6*

his birthday, October 1, 1997. "Mom, Smoochy's birthday is the same day as my next surgery! Did your friend know when my surgery was scheduled?"

"No, dear, I never mentioned the date," I replied. I was sure that the store-owner had no idea when Kody's surgery was scheduled. He just picked a Beanie off the shelf and tossed it to Kody. I got goosebumps thinking about it.

Kody smiled. "Mom, I think this is a sign that everything will come out fine in my surgery."

I nodded and smiled, too, blinking back tears.

Kody took Smoochy with him to the hospital. It never left his bedside. He said, "I'll always keep this Beanie close. Smoochy means so much to me."

The surgery was successful. Today we are so thankful for special friends—real and stuffed.

# What Are You Going to Do with All Those Beanie Babies?

## BY DIANNE E. BUTTS

❤ ❤ ❤

**G**ail owns a specialty shop, and one of her featured items is Beanie Babies. She enjoys watching her customers' reactions to various Beanies. In watching their buying habits, Gail has noticed many Beanie Baby buyers have certain things in common.

Most of her customers are women. After selecting their Beanies and bringing them to the register, many make the same comment. While opening their wallets, they lean over the counter and whisper sheepishly, "Do you know how many of these things I already own? And now I'm spending more money on them! Ya know, my husband's gonna kill me!"

Gail just smiles knowingly as she takes their money and sends them on their way with their latest purchases.

Gail has a friend in a nearby town, who also owns a shop that sells Beanie Babies. Most of Hannah's Beanie lovers are also women. Over the phone, she and Hannah have often discussed the habits of Beanie buyers, and the storeowners have discovered a similarity between many of their clients.

Hannah often asks her customers, "What are you going to do with all those Beanie Babies?"

The typical customer looks this way and that to see if anyone is watching. Then she quietly confesses, "I'm going to stick them under the bed with all the others where my husband won't find them!"

*Sheri Gonzalez, age 12*

The two storeowners have enjoyed exchanging stories as they compare their buyers. Yet, one day the tables were turned for Gail when a gentleman came into her store. He wasn't familiar with Beanie Babies, but when he saw the adorable little critters, he chose several to take home.

He took them to the register, but glanced back longingly at the display rack. Leaving his cuddly critters in a heap on the counter, he went back to the rack and selected more. When Gail finally totaled his bill, he leaned over the counter and quietly said, "Ya know, my wife is gonna kill me!"

# Carissa's Gift

## BY CATHLEEN SHINEW

❤ ❤ ❤

**M**y daughter Carissa has been collecting Beanies for a year or so. Her favorites are, of course, the bears. She takes good care of them and keeps them up on the shelf, being careful not to damage the tags.

When my husband and I told her we were having another baby, she wasn't quite sure if she wanted another brother or sister. She already had two brothers. Throughout the pregnancy she acted like it was no big deal. That all changed though when the baby came, and Carissa learned it was a girl.

The second she saw Michaela Grace she fell in love.

When we brought Michaela home, Carissa was sitting in a chair waiting to hold her. After everything settled down I decided to lay Michaela in her bassinet. There I found Princess, Valentino, and Gracie without tags.

Surprised, I asked Carissa, "Why did you put them there?"

She replied, "They are gifts for Michaela. I gave her Valentino because I love my new baby sister. Princess is there because Michaela is the new "Princess" in the family.

And I gave her Gracie because her middle name is Grace.

"That's really special," I said, "But why did you take the tags off?"

She answered, "Mom, you should know that babies can choke on things like that!"

All I could do was laugh through my tears. I hugged her and told her she was an angel. She said, "If they made an angel Beanie, I would give her that, too."

That incident happened two months ago. Since then, Carissa has taught me all about Beanie Babies. Now, we go Beanie hunting together, and we have started a collection for Michaela.

Ty must have been reading her mind because he did come out with an angel bear named Halo. Guess what is at the top of Carissa's wish list?

I am truly blessed with a generous child.

*Rex Mackall*

# The Beanie Romance

## BY ERIC GONGORA

I was introduced to Beanie Babies about the same time that a special woman came into my life, although I didn't give much thought to either at the time. I had received a Beanie named Coral from a friend and had placed the fish on a shelf in my office. I thought it was cute, but I wasn't aware of the Beanie craze or that Beanie Babies had become collector items.

A casual friend stopped by my office and admired Coral. She mentioned that some people were paying lots of money for Beanies. We both were interested in finding out more about this hobby, and we decided to explore it together. We started finding Beanie Web sites on the Internet. If either of us found a special deal or heard of a retirement, we would call the other at work.

We even made a weekly ritual of going to breakfast at the Cracker Barrel and buying a few Beanies together. Then we started going to McDonald's on occasion to get Teenie Beanies. The relationship progressed, and we began getting together to show each other our latest Beanies.

Before we knew it, we had become quite close. Not only

*Taylor Osborn, age 7½*

were we interested in Beanies, but we were interested in each other, too. We started dating over a year ago, and we are now engaged.

I knew from the beginning of our dating relationship that we would be together for a very long time. We had started out as friends, and that wonderful friendship grew into a romance we never expected. I would definitely say that Beanies helped bring us together. We now have a large collection of over one hundred Beanie Babies and are quite obsessed.

It is truly amazing what a few pieces of fabric sewn together and filled with pellets can do. Next year we are planning a wedding, and Beanie Babies will surely be a part of it.

# Popular Peking

BY JULIE STANGLER

♥ ♥ ♥

As an American living in the Philippines, I had not been home for almost a year. When I returned for a summer visit and sat down to enjoy dinner with my family, the conversation eventually turned to Beanie Babies. I already knew that Beanie Babies were cute little beanbag animals, and each one had his or her own name. I had even bought a Beanie Baby while traveling in China. But I was surprised to hear how the Beanie Baby craze had overtaken America.

In the past several months I have discovered a great deal about Beanie Babies. I learned that they not only have little tags on their ears and rears (technically called "tush tags"), but there are also generations, birthdates, and "retired" Beanies. (Can "retired" Beanie Babies collect Social Security and other retirement benefits?) I also learned that they are virtually worthless if the tags have been removed. Books, magazines, and catalogs are available for the serious Beanie Baby fan, as well as collectors' fairs and swap meets where normal looking adults spend the weekend comparing, buying, and selling lovable stuffed critters. America is a strange and wonderful place!

The more I learned about Beanie Babies, the more I realized I might have a lucrative investment in the cuddly bear I purchased in China. While there, I picked up Peking the panda, and, to my surprise, discovered that Peking is one of the top two retired bears most in demand.

My sister, Maureen, who knows as little about Beanie Babies as I do, volunteered to take Peking to a local Beanie Baby show to see what it was worth. As she entered the crowded room full of Beanie fans, she looked around for another panda in order to determine its current value. But none were to be found. Finally Maureen removed the bear from her purse and asked one of the dealers what it was worth. As Maureen looked up she suddenly noticed that the room had grown still, and all eyes were staring at her.

"The woman in the blue jacket has a Peking bear," echoed all over the room. A large man wearing a Green Bay Packers shirt stepped forward and said, "Lady, when you took that bear out of your purse I thought my heart would stop." Everyone pushed around her, anxious to be near the panda.

"Could I see the bear?" they asked. "Can I touch it?"

"Where did you get it?" they wanted to know. Maureen panicked and quickly headed toward the car. A man in the parking lot offered her $500 for the Beanie Baby. She hurried home with Peking safely tucked away in her purse.

After Maureen's disastrous foray into the world of Beanie collectors, we decided we needed to do further research in order to make an intelligent decision about Peking's future. Several of Maureen's friends provided us with information about counterfeit Beanie Babies. It made me wonder: *What would happen if we sold little Peking only to find that he was a fake? Would we be charged with a Beanie Baby felony? Would the man in the Green Bay Packer shirt come after us some dark night for trying to pass off a fake Beanie Baby?*

Just before my visit ended, I took Peking to the Mall of America in Minneapolis, Minnesota. It was there that Beanie Baby experts looked him over and pronounced him "real." In *The Velveteen Rabbit* a toy only becomes real when it is well loved! When the experts suggested a $2,000 price tag for the little panda I suddenly fell very much in love with Peking! As I laughed and told them no one would ever pay $2,000 for a little beanbag toy, a woman at the other counter was just completing her transaction. You can imagine my amazement when the clerk explained that she had just paid $2,500(cash)for a Beanie Baby elephant! All I can say is Americans are crazy!

> The Canadian tush tags have words in both English and French.

# Bonkers for Beanies

## BY LIZ CURTIS HIGGS

❤ ❤ ❤

I was slicing carrots when my eight-year-old daughter, Lillian, tucked a note in my pocket before disappearing in the direction of the family room. Curious, I wiped off my hands and opened the tightly folded paper.

"Dear Mom," the message began. "For Christmas I want Velvet, Flip, Chip, Nip, Zip, Stripes, Derby, Wrinkles, and Congo."

I scratched my head. "She wants *what*?"

So began my introduction to the brave new world of Beanie Mania. I groan when I think of the months that I ignored these droopy little animals stuffed with plastic pellets.

But that was last year. This year, I've lurked in the corners of Hallmark stores, staring at the empty bins as if suddenly—magically—a pile of Pinchers (the Lobster) would appear before my eyes. (I haven't gone so far as to follow delivery men through the mall, hoping their precious cargo included Inky or Stinky, but on several occasions we did pull up to the curb of a local gift shop, only to find a sign in the window bearing the sad tidings: *Sorry. We're Out of Beanies.*)

*Julianne Rucker, age 12*

On one memorable occasion, I was in the right place at the right time. Standing inside a nature store in Suttons Bay, Michigan, during off-season, I found a gaggle of giggling elementary children gathered around a display wall with dozens of empty slots. *What in the world is this about?* I wondered, then spied a small, hand-lettered sign: *Beanies will arrive between Noon and 2:00.*

I glanced at my watch. Nearly 1:00 p.m. and obviously no Beanies in sight. Could I possibly kill an hour in such a tiny store, trying to look nonchalant like all those other parents standing among the birdhouses and sundials, pretending to be shopping when in truth they were waiting for a kind man with a large cardboard box to show up and make their children deliriously happy?

Suddenly the storeowner strolled in from the stockroom, welcomed by squeals of delight. And that was just the parents! The kids were practically hyperventilating, wiggling like puppies, nearly knocking over the nice man with the box.

*Limit Four* the sign said, so I dutifully chose the allotted amount and headed for the cash register, embarrassed to be part of the frenzy.

"Only four?" the clerk said, surprised.

"Isn't that the limit?"

"Oh no," she insisted, shaking her head. "It's four of each kind. You're welcome to take more."

But when I turned, less than thirty seconds after the box had been opened, it was empty, and a long line of parents with booty in hand were waiting for me to cough up the loot and scoot. I paid and headed for my car, mumbling over my mistake, yet grateful to be heading home with such a treasure.

So there's the ugly, sordid truth of it: I've become as captivated by Beanie Mania as my children are. Is there a 12-step group for this? Beanies Anonymous, perhaps?

As a mother of two, I've fought such brand-name toy nonsense for years. Who do those suits in New York or Hollywood think they are, telling my children what's hot and what's not? Harruummph. We were the last—*the last*—family in our church to break down and buy a Nintendo system. We breezed right past Tickle Me Elmo last Christmas without batting a dollar. Thankfully, our children were born post-Cabbage Patch and pre-Barney, so we were spared any hoopla with those two trendsetters.

However, 1997 will be remembered as the year that even

those of us who love the Lord and hate marketplace manipulation might have succumbed to a certain fondness for the little critters with the heart-shaped tags.

Which brings me to Lesson One: *Do not cut off the tag!* When I brought home the first of many Beanies, I snipped off the tag and disposed of it, sending my children scurrying through the trashcan and fretting over how to reattach the little red heart.

"You've ruined the resale value, Mom!" they moaned. *Resale* value! Where did they learn a concept like that? I thought I was just bringing them an inexpensive toy, not a squeezable contribution for their college fund. Hmmmm.

Who could have imagined the inventive activities these little toys would inspire? And they're a natural for birthday parties, because *they all have birthdays*! Not just a specific year, but month and day, too.

But if there are Beanies in the room, don't even think about serving a gooey, chocolate birthday cake, thanks to Lesson Two: *Do not throw them in the washing machine!* Wrap them in plastic on rainy days, and keep them out of mud puddles at all costs. The plus side: Beanies provide the perfect motivation for children who need a reason to wash their hands more than once a week.

As an adult with other things on my mind, I find it hard to keep track of them all. Hippity, Hoppity, and Floppity are bunnies—mint-green, pink, and lavender, respectively—but Pinky is a flamingo that comes in two sizes, and Lucky is a ladybug that comes in *three* official versions—all with anti-lottery messages.

With Beanies, it's been Christmas all year at our house. The total tally is twenty-one—ridiculous, of course—though I console myself with the fact that there are more than 150 out there to choose from, they're inexpensive, and I've never paid a dime above retail (though I'd entertain any reasonable price for that illusive Velvet).

What's a mother to do? "Refuse to play the game" is the obvious solution. Yet, when I watched a mere six-dollar gift bring a huge smile to my daughter's face, and stimulate an entire day of creative play, it's hard to put my foot down on so soft a present.

Don't laugh, but I've even thought of the Scripture, "Which of you fathers, if your son asks for a fish, will give him a snake instead?" (Luke 11:11 NIV). Of course, the Lord was hardly referring to Bubbles and Slither. But the point of his lesson still applies here: Parents who love their children give them what they want and need most, which challenges me to find the proper response, even about something as trivial and finite as a pile of floppy stuffed animals.

Even as I write this, I rationalize. I find myself unable to resist the certain sense of pride and satisfaction they bring to *me*, the giver. It's the $5.99 way to say, "I love you," plastic beans and all.

But God's Word is there to help me sweep away my hypocrisy: "Anyone, then, who knows the good he ought to do and doesn't do it, sins"(James 4:17 NIV). There you have it. For me, the good and right thing to do is to find more meaningful ways to show my kids how much I love them. Not with dollars, but with words. Not with Beanies, but with hugs.

When the next fad comes along, I pray I'm ready with a better response, knowing that one of the greatest gifts I can give my children is free, yet costly: time, and my undivided attention. My own heart-shaped tag will also be permanently attached, as I give my children the gift they want most, complete with this original poem:

Tall and lumpy, sometimes frumpy
Trying hard not to be grumpy
Glad I am that I'm your mother
Who adores you like no other!

"Bonkers for Beanies" first appeared in the November/ December 1997 issue of *Today's Christian Woman.* Used with permission of the author.

# More Beanie Baby® Stories

💜 💜 💜

💜 Would you like to have your Beanie Baby story included in our next book?

💜 If so e-mail or write us for guidelines.

💜 If you'd like to learn to polish your writing skills, e-mail or write for a free brochure on our writing courses and resources.

For guidelines and/or a free brochure contact:

Susan Titus Osborn & Sandra Jensen
3133 Puente Street
Fullerton CA 92835
Susanosb@aol.com
www.christiancommunicator.com

**SUSAN TITUS OSBORN** is a contributing editor of *The Christian Communicator* magazine. Susan is also an adjunct professor at Hope International University. She has authored eighteen books and numerous articles, devotionals, and curriculum materials. Susan has taught at over 110 writers' conferences across the US and in five foreign countries. She is listed in Marquis *Who's Who in America, Who's Who of American Women, Who's Who in the World, Who's Who in the West, and Who's Who in the Media and Communications.* E-mail Susan at Susanosb@aol.com.

**SANDRA JENSEN** is a contributing editor for *World View*, a periodical devoted to the stories of missionaries around the world. In addition, she is an editor for the Christian Communicator Manuscript Critique Service. Sandra also writes material for Christian broadcasting as well as various missionary agencies. Sandra previously served as assistant editor of *The Christian Communicator* and as a contributing editor of *Trails 'N' Treasures* magazine.

# Books by Starburst Publishers®

❤ ❤ ❤

**Beanie Baby® Stories**
*Compiled by Susan Titus Osborn and Sandra Jensen*

Adults and children share their stories, illustrations, and trivia about those collectable, lovable, squeezable Beanie Babies. Includes essays from acclaimed writers like Liz Curtis Higgs and Karen O'Connor. A book that will surely touch your heart, just as Beanie Babies have!

(trade paper)   ISBN 1892016044   **$10.95**


**Seasons of a Woman's Heart—A Daybook of Stories and Inspiration**
*Compiled by Lynn D. Morrissey*

A woman's heart is complex. This daybook of stories, quotes, scriptures, and daily reflections will inspire and refresh. Christian women share their heart-felt thoughts on Seasons of Faith, Growth, Guidance, Nurturing, and Victory. Including Christian women's writers such as Kay Arthur, Emilie Barnes, Luci Swindoll, Jill Briscoe, Florence Littauer, and Gigi Graham Tchividjian.

(cloth)   ISBN 1892016036   **$18.95**

## Why Fret That God Stuff?
*Edited by Kathy Collard Miller*

Subtitled: *Stories of Encouragement to Help You Let Go and Let God Take Control of All Things in Your Life.* Occasionally, we all become overwhelmed by the everyday challenges of our lives: hectic schedules, our loved ones' needs, unexpected expenses, a sagging devotional life. *Why Fret That God Stuff* is the perfect beginning to finding joy and peace for the real world!

(trade paper)   ISBN 0914984-500   **$12.95**

The *God's Vitamin "C" for the Spirit*™ series has already sold over 250,000 copies! Jam-packed with stories from well-known Christian writers that will enlighten your spirits and enrich your life!

## God's Vitamin "C" for the Spirit™
*Kathy Collard Miller & D. Larry Miller*

Subtitled: *"Tug-at-the-Heart" Stories to Fortify and Enrich Your Life.* Includes inspiring stories and anecdotes that emphasize Christian ideals and values by Barbara Johnson, Billy Graham, Nancy L. Dorner, and many other well-known Christian speakers and writers. Topics include: Love, Family Life, Faith and Trust, Prayer, and God's Guidance.

(trade paper)   ISBN 0914984837   **$12.95**

### God's Vitamin "C" for the Spirit™ of Women
*Kathy Collard Miller*

Subtitled: *"Tug-at-the-Heart" Stories to Inspire and Delight Your Spirit*. A beautiful treasury of timeless stories, quotes, and poetry designed by and for women. Well-known Christian women like Liz Curtis Higgs, Patsy Clairmont, Naomi Rhode, and Elisabeth Elliot share from their hearts on subjects like Marriage, Motherhood, Christian Living, Faith, and Friendship.

(trade paper)   ISBN 0914984934   **$12.95**

### God's Vitamin "C" for the Hurting Spirit™
*Kathy Collard Miller & D. Larry Miller*

The latest in the best-selling *God's Vitamin "C" for the Spirit* series, this collection of real-life stories expresses the breadth and depth of God's love for us in our times of need. Rejuvenating and inspiring thoughts from some of the most-loved Christian writers such as Max Lucado, Cynthia Heald, Charles Swindoll, and Barbara Johnson. Topics include: Death, Divorce/Separation, Financial Loss, and Physical Illness.

(trade paper)   ISBN 0914984691   **$12.95**

## God's Vitamin "C" for the Christmas Spirit
*Kathy Collard Miller & D. Larry Miller*

Subtitled: *"Tug-at-the-Heart" Traditions and Inspirations to Warm the Heart.* This keepsake includes a variety of heart-tugging thoughts, stories, poetry, recipes, songs, and crafts.

(cloth)    ISBN 0914984853    **$14.95**

# Purchasing Information
### www.starburstpublishers.com

Books are available from your favorite bookstore, either from current stock or special order. To assist bookstores in locating your selection, be sure to give title, author, and ISBN. If unable to purchase from the bookstore, you may order direct from STARBURST PUBLISHERS. When ordering enclose full payment plus shipping and handling as follows: Post Office (4th Class)—$3.00 (Up to $20.00), $4.00 ($20.01-$50.00), 8% ($50.01 and Up); UPS—$4.50 (Up to $20.00), $6.00 ($20.01-$50.00), 12% ($50.01 and Up); Canada—$5.00 (Up to $35.00), 15% ($35.01 and Up); Overseas (Surface)—$5.00 (Up to $25.00), 20% ($25.01 and Up). Payment in U.S. Funds only. Please allow two to three weeks minimum (longer overseas) for delivery. Make checks payable to and mail to:

STARBURST PUBLISHERS
P.O. Box 4123
Lancaster, PA 17604

Credit card orders may also be placed by calling 1-800-441-1456 (credit card orders only), Mon-Fri, 8:30 a.m. to 5:30 p.m. Eastern Standard Time. Prices subject to change without notice. Catalog available for a 9 x 12 self-addressed envelope with four first-class stamps.